D1488989

Curiosities of
WINE

In friendship and with respect
this book is dedicated to The Society of Authors
and especially to
Miss Jo Hodder, whose good sense and charm
are much appreciated

Curiosities of WINE

Clinking, Drinking and the Extras that Surround the Bottles

PAMELA VANDYKE PRICE

Foreword by
OZ CLARKE

SUTTON PUBLISHING

First published in the United Kingdom in 2002 by
Sutton Publishing Limited · Phoenix Mill
Thrupp · Stroud · Gloucestershire · GL5 2BU

British Library Cataloguing in Publication Data
A catalogue record for this book is available from the British
Library.

ISBN 0-7509-2754-2

Typeset in 11/16pt Photina.
Typesetting and origination by
Sutton Publishing Limited.
Printed and bound in England by
J.H. Haynes & Co. Ltd, Sparkford.

CONTENTS

FOREWORD

I blame it all on Pamela. There I was, with a nice little Theology and Psychology degree tucked under my belt wondering what was the quickest way to become a Bishop – claret, nice purple shirt, palace of your own, very appealing – and then I met Pamela. I'd just emerged victorious from a bruising duel in the annual Oxford–Cambridge wine-tasting match and was feeling pretty pleased with myself when up floated this vision in aquamarine and bluntly asked, 'So what do you intend to do in life?' I don't know what came over me – but then, many others fixed with Pamela's questioning gaze over the years could say the same – so I blurted out: I want to be a wine writer. There was a very silent pause as she gave me the most old-fashioned of looks – Pamela has quite a collection of old-fashioned looks; I got top drawer right from the start – and then she said, 'Mmmmm. Prudent be. Prudent be.'

At the time Pamela was the most influential wine writer in Britain, proudly female in a very male world, determinedly radical and freethinking in a wine community stifling in its conservatism. She was a populist whose way with words immediately struck a chord with her readers as well as being a highly erudite expert on such citadels of tradition as the great wine regions of Germany and France. And she was busy. But she wrote up the tasting in her *Spectator* column, and mentioned this cocky young student and his ambitions to write. And that could have been the end of it. But Pamela wasn't like that.

I received a note from her at my college. If you really want to be a wine writer, she wrote, every month I'll take you to a tasting in London, I'll introduce you to the great and the good; I'll show you the different styles of wine the world can offer. And I'll make you have an opinion. And she did. Every month I'd turn up with my hair combed and my tie straight. 'What times', she'd cry, 'What times!' and she'd usher me into the hallowed halls of wine – one month Claret, the next Sherries, then maybe Hock and Mosel, Ports, Alsace and Champagne. She'd chaperone me for a little while, then cut me free, to sink or swim as best I could before later testing my new knowledge and demanding my opinions.

These early introductions and those challenging tastings were enough to set me on my path. And as I grew more confident I got to know Pamela better and better and appreciate her not only for her unique personality which could thrill you or chill you entirely according to her whim. But I also realised what a vast repository she was of knowledge – facts, figures, fantasies and inspired foolishness about every facet of wine, from the beginning of wine time to the lurid imaginings of the uncharted future.

And as such she is a perfect person to write about the Curiosities of Wine. Chatty, gossipy, flirtatious, arch, waspish and droll. What an irresistible bundle of contradictions. She'll lead you in and out of the highways and byways of wine with the same sure touch of literary brilliance that has entranced all of her fans over so many years.

Oz Clarke

PREFACE

This book is not directly about wine, but about the various traditions, associated objects and personalities who have been much influenced by wine or wines. Rather curiously, a number of words and phrases to do with wine do not get into the large books of reference so it has been interesting to research such things in the background to wine and the changing fashions in drinking, plus the multitude of accessories that have been created to enable people to gain greater enjoyment from wine.

Although sources have been acknowledged wherever possible, in the course of more than fifty years of studying wine it is inevitable that some things have just been 'known', picked up when talking to wine people, or given in the form of instruction from a variety of men and women in various regions of the wine world. A bibliography in one of my earlier books runs to ten pages on wines and it would seem unnecessary for this to be repeated. Every week, sometimes every day, new discoveries are publicised about wine – it is to be hoped this will always be so! Many aspects of wine are long-lasting; none should be static or assumed to be 'right' as long as sensible drinkers have free will and use their intelligence.

Two things not dealt with in this book include spirits – that is a subject in itself and there are many good reference books on spirits in particular and in general. The other is drunkenness and excess in drinking. There are books about this, just as there are books about excesses in sex, eating, physical achievements of various kinds. Human beings are individuals and what may be pleasant, disgusting or overwhelming to one, may be a delight, a rewarding hobby or a form of anaesthesia to others. The human intelligence needs to relate people to circumstances, because generalisations are risky. I cannot be expected to eat and drink as once I did – although in some ways I know my capacity better than I did fifty years ago! Even the challenge of finding out what you do and no longer enjoy is stimulating.

For wine is a stimulant – to all the senses. Wine lovers are usually active and lively in mind whether they live long or are 'whom the gods love' and die young. Wine is and should be fun – not a snob or show-off subject; it keeps some of us young – and not too serious!

Pamela Vandyke Price
2002

ONE

DEFINITIONS, ORIGINS AND ANCIENT LEGENDS

WINE: DEFINITIONS

This is possibly the most important section in this book. It comes from The Wine and Spirit Association of Great Britain, which nowadays organises courses in many countries throughout the world. They say that the two languages they use most in teaching are German and Japanese – this, of course, is because so many wish to enter the catering trade and work internationally – but French is much used as well. No traveller should be affronted should a sommelier in a Spanish-speaking country offer some 'Champaña'

Judging Chardonnay wines at the California State Fair. (*Mick Rock/Cephas*)

when a perfectly acceptable 'cava' may actually be served – the niceties of nomenclature need not affect the drinker or customer in a bar; he or she should always ask to see the bottle and interpret its label if there is any doubt as to what is being offered. However strict regulations are, there will always be those who put their own interpretations on to certain terms.

The official definition of wine is:

> The alcoholic beverage obtained from the juice of freshly gathered grapes, the fermentation of which has been carried through in the district of its origin and according to local tradition and practice.

This means that alcoholic beverages made from fruits other than grapes, from, say, imported dried grapes, imported musts or, of course, fruits other than grapes are not wines. (What went on in POW camps, when amazing drinks were fabricated from fantastic sources do not comply with the United Kingdom definition of wine.) Any fruit that can undergo fermentation can make an alcoholic beverage. It isn't 'wine'.

Fortified Wine

This is, as the name implies, 'made stronger' than ordinary table wine (though one should always look at the label). Additions to the great classic wines of port, sherry and even Malaga and Marsala are examples.

Unless the drinker is in a very obscure region, the alcoholic strength will be stated on the label.

Never suppose that you can be sure of the strength of any wine just by trying it. You may be experienced – you may obtain a definite impression as to the strength of the drink. But many things may influence and affect your taste – don't rely on it! If you are not familiar with the wines of a region or country, look at the label, or when possible, check the alcoholic content of your drink. If this is impossible, a very moderate sniff or sip is advisable.

YEAST

 This is the driving force that makes wine and creates life. There are various kinds, the wine yeast *Saccharomyces cerevisae* being the most important. Wild yeasts are slightly different and the whole subject is somewhat technical. The important thing to remember is that if it rains at vintage time the yeasts are washed off the ripening grapes. But yeasts have always existed and the work of Louis Pasteur enabled at least some of their variety and achievements to be understood.

In high and low temperatures, yeasts cannot work for if dead yeasts – for they are living things – are left in wine, this will become vinegar.

Anyone able to visit a winery may fall silent at seeing the way in which the surface of the wine quivers during the fermentation. In a sherry cask there may be a coating of 'flor' over the wine or, sometimes, just a minute piece of 'fluff' in one corner. It is impressive, even intimidating. For this is life.

WHERE DID WINE BEGIN?

 There is no answer that is definite, although there are many theories. Fermented drinks certainly seem to have evolved millennia ago, but wine, from grapes, is still a mysterious commodity. Some have supposed that a Mediterranean shepherd forgot a bunch of grapes and left them to ferment in the sun. There they were found by a distraught woman, cast out from the Sultan's nearby harem, who supposed that she would die if she ate them. On the contrary! The lady not only enjoyed the sweet juice but, on returning to the Sultan's palace, her appearance and liveliness were so apparent that she regained favour and recovered the status she had lost.

It is possible that grapes grew and thrived even before the advent of man. The vine may have first shown itself around the Caspian Sea and the most ancient Greek and Egyptian records mention it. It is also, of course, featured in the Book of Genesis, when 'Noah began to be an husbandman' and planted a vineyard, with disastrous results for himself.

The most common wine grape is *Vitis vinifera*, although there are numerous others, including many native to America. The grape provided a pleasant source of nourishment and records for its use in wine can be traced to six thousand years ago. Not only is the grape pleasant to eat and able to quench thirst, but it has digestive properties, contains both glucose and fructose, and Vitamins C and B Complex. Grapes grown solely for the production of wine are not usually very

The Egyptians picked, sorted and, sometimes, dried grapes for increased yields of sugar. The arcades of vines would also have provided shade for those who spent as much time out of doors as possible. Detail from a wall painting from the Tomb of Nakht, New Kingdom. (*Valley of the Nobles, Egypt/Bridgeman Art Library*)

agreeable to eat, because of their thick skins and, often, small size. Dried grapes or raisins feature in many of the regional recipes around the Mediterranean and the way in which raisins can be kept does, of course, make them a valuable source of food in winter. The tradition of taking grapes when visiting an invalid relates to the valuable nutritional properties the fruit provides even when only taken in small amounts.

In pre-Christian times, the way in which the God of Wine might take possession of some of the worshippers was considered of importance as a type of divine frenzy. Christian saints, however, often turned worshippers away from frenzy to ecstasy, and with the centuries, it became less usual for Christians of the established faith in England to make the frequent Communions – involving sharing the cup – of former times.

But wine and the shared cup featured in many religious rituals before Christianity; indeed, to decline to drink with anyone with whom a meal or social occasion was shared was, and still is, a rebuff; to refuse to share even a soft drink is, discourteous and, of course, in the past, the refusal of a shared drink could imply that the commodity was suspect.

HOW THE CLINK GOT INTO THE DRINK

 Once on Mount Olympus there was trouble among the gods and goddesses. The seven senses had been asked to a party by Dionysus, God of Wine, but even the most delectable beverages his butler, Bacchus, poured with a lavish hand, couldn't make them all happy. The senses – at least six of them – expressed satisfaction in being able to contribute to wine sessions. Animation lit up the eyes and encouraged people to dance around. The sense of Feeling spent much time sucking up mouthfuls of wine, nodding wisely and exchanging opinion with the sense of Speech, who was occupied with a notebook – they might have been a couple of wine writers. The sense of Taste went in for lip-smacking and satisfied expressions after swallowing, looking somewhat disdainfully at the sense of Sight, who held a glass up to the sunshine, and the sense of Smell, who made noises rather like a piglet sniffing at some delicious fruit or flower. All the senses were busy – except one. This was a grumpy-looking person who wasn't drinking at all and went up to Dionysus in an attitude of one about to complain.

'You always leave me out! Everyone else can get something from wine, not me – how can I hear it?' For this was the sense of Hearing.

'You could, of course,' said Dionysus jovially, 'get yourself into a winery when the wine is beginning to make itself: the guggling, plopping, surging sounds – these should please you.'

'But I can't just stay there!' objected Hearing. 'You all have a fine time around the table; unless somebody breaks a glass or drops down drunk, there's nothing for me there!' Dionysus seized one glass from Bacchus who nudged Hearing so that he took another.

'Now listen! Whenever people get together to enjoy wine they will do this –' and he brought his glass up against that of Hearing, so that both of them rang pleasantly. 'See?' said the God of Wine. 'Whether it's glass against glass, beaker against beaker, crock against crock – this is the music of those who love wine! Cheers!' The sense of Hearing was quite surprised and went round clashing his glass against all the others until Juno sent Dionysus a message that there was so much glass on the floor that the ladies wanted it cleared away in case they hurt their feet, and would he give an extra tip to Charon, who was usually quite amiable about dumping empties in the Styx, but so much splintered glass might be bad for the fish. . . .

So, that is one version as to how the clink got into the drink.

The Oldest Disinfectant?

 In the parable of 'The Good Samaritan' in the New Testament, it is related that the man who 'fell among thieves' had his wounds washed with wine and dressed with oil. From earliest times soldiers on duty in regions not their own would carry basic equipment for eating, including a cup of some kind. This was not only for routine drinking but so that they could add a little wine to the water of any strange pond or stream to counteract any 'bugs'. Often, the inhabitants of an area might be able to drink the local water supply without harm, but for strangers there could be an adverse reaction. (It has been reported that a certain very important royal lady always has a lavish supply of her preferred mineral water when she travels.) Indeed, when I first began to go abroad after the Second World War I felt quite audacious when I actually drank the tap water in a famous resort!

There are, of course, other forms of disinfectant. In *The Seven Pillars of Wisdom*, Colonel T.E. Lawrence records how the Arabs, when attacking the Turks, would take their boyfriends with them on their camels, not just for company but so that, if anyone were wounded, a 'clean-living boy' could urinate on to the wound, the acidity thereby disinfecting it.

One wine that attracted the attention of the bucks and dandies of the Regency period in Britain, because they wanted their top boots to gleam like looking-glasses, was Champagne, which was tried in the mixture with which the valets cleaned the boots. If you should spill some Champagne or fairly dry sparkling wine on to the floor, it will be noticed how, in wiping up the liquid any grease is removed from the flooring – hence the use of Champagne in the 'blacking' of the dandies' boots.

SAINTS OF WINE

Since records began, there have been those who might be supposed to look beneficently upon wine and those who grew and made it. Dionysus was the Greek god of vegetation, ecstasy and wine, being the son of Zeus by Semele. Bacchus, on the other hand, was the wine god for the Romans. The effect of wine on drinkers was thought to be magical, associated with a divine influence.

Dionysus has, however, undergone a curious rehabilitation. There was a Dionysus of Alexandria in the second century AD, but not much seems to be known about him. Shortly after this, under the name of **Denis** or Denys, another Dionysus was sent as a missionary into Gaul at the end of the second century. He was

Bacchus was the Roman god of wine but all the fruits of the field were under his auspices. Note the backpack or grape-picker's carrier and the way in which he drinks from the kylix before watering the soil. Engraving by Crispin de Passe I, *c.* 1565–1637. (*Private collection/Bridgeman Art Library*)

beheaded at Martyrs' Hill – the modern Montmartre, but as the *Penguin Dictionary of Saints* states, three quite different people, living at different times, seem to have been 'made into one man'. But the legend mainly associated with him was that, after being beheaded, he carried his head to where he was buried, the abbey associated with his name – The Abbey of Saint Denys or Denis – where subsequent kings of France have always been buried. A famous quip associated with this occurred when a discussion was held among some learned Frenchmen about the distance St Denys walked to the Abbey, which was considerable. At which, one sharpwittedly commented, 'Dans les tels circonstances, ce n'est que le premier pas qui coûte.' (At such a time, it's only the first step that matters.) St Denis is the patron saint of France. His feast is celebrated on 9 October. The celebration of St Denis, at what might be the beginning of the vintage, is naturally of major importance.

Among the other numerous saints, it is only possible to include a few relating to wine and not much is known about many of these. The '**Ice Saints**' that can come into conversation among members of the wine trade are Pancratius, Servatius, Boniface and Sophid. Their festivals occur during the middle of May, a time when, in the northern hemisphere, vineyards may be at risk from sudden frosts. These days they do not seem to be celebrated, but they are certainly noted!

Other saints celebrate festivals in what might be the dark days of winter.

Medieval depiction of St Denis preaching, with a portrayal of the church where the sovereigns of France were buried. (*Bibliothèque Nationale, Paris/Bridgeman Art Library*)

The martyr **Vincent of Saragossa** was put to death under Diocletian in 304. His feast day is 22 January. He is a patron of Spain and of French wine growers; in fact, his fame spread to England, where some churches seem to have been dedicated to him. Visitors to a great Graves property in the Bordeaux area may be told of the tradition that on one occasion Vincent delayed his return to heaven – and was found lingering in the *chais* of Haut Brion.

Urbain, Bishop of Autun, is the patron of German wine growers. There seem to have been two martyrs of this name, but 25 May seems to be associated with the wine saint. **Cyriak** is the patron of Franconian growers in the Palatinate. **Kilian**, who died in 689, was Bishop of Wurzburg. His festival is 8 July and is celebrated in Wurzburg, Vienna and Ireland.

The most famous wine saint, however, is probably **Martin of Tours**. Martin's dates are *c*. 316–97. He was born in what is now Hungary, grew up in Pavia, and, like his father, went into the army; he became increasingly dissatisfied as a faithful Christian with his service as a soldier. The most famous of the stories associated with him occurred when, at Amiens, a beggar asked him for alms. Martin had no money to bestow but he cut his cloak in half, so as to give it to the beggar – and, that night, Jesus appeared in a dream to tell Martin to whom he had given the half of the cloak. After this, Martin left the army, took up serious study and became the pioneer of western monasticism, being made Bishop of Tours in 372, and founding what was to be the first monastery in Gaul, at Marmoutier nearby.

The association of Martin with wine occurs then, for he took a party of monks on their asses out to work in the vine-yards and it was noted with dismay later that the untethered animals had nibbled the shoots of

St Martin of Tours, shown having cut off half his cloak for the beggar who importuned him for alms – but who was Christ in disguise. Detail from the Breviary of John the Fearless, *c.* 1415, Harl. 2897 f. 435. (*British Library, London/Bridgeman Art Library*)

the nearby vines. However, at the forthcoming vintage, it was seen that these vines had grown stronger and produced finer fruit! In fact, this cannot be more than a charming tale, because the cultivation of the vine and methods of pruning were known to the Romans.

This saint is of great popularity in wine regions: in France there are about 500 parishes associated with his name and 5,000 churches; there are also parishes and churches dedicated to him in Germany, Spain, Italy and The Netherlands. In Britain there are many churches dedicated to him, notably St Martin-in-the-Fields, so tagged because it was outside the boundary of the City of London. The Vintners' Company also have Martin as their patron.

Martin's festival is 11 November. The term 'St Martin's Summer' is often given to the spell of fine weather that occurs around this time. According to the *Oxford Dictionary of Saints*, this was the time when people would hire servants to prepare for the feasts at the turn of the year and it was also the period when many domestic animals were killed preparatory to being salted and put into store for the winter.

Benedict, 'patriarch of Western monks', is another saint who must be associated with wine. Although it does not seem that he ever became a priest, his Rule (*c.* 540 AD) stated, 'We read that wine is not suitable for monks. But because, in our day, it is not possible to persuade monks of this, let us agree at least that we should not drink to excess. We believe that one pint of wine is enough.' A recent scholar interprets that the daily allowance would have been about half a litre of wine – in accordance with Benedict's wish that there should be 'nothing harsh or rigorous' in his Rule. It is possibly significant of this practical and humane man that, apparently, he died standing up and was buried in the same grave as his sister, St Scholastica. His feast is 21 March.

DOMITIAN'S DECREE

Roman Emperor from AD 81 to 96, Domitian was one of the two sons of the great Emperor Vespasian, younger brother of Titus, the commander responsible for the wars in Germany and the Middle East. He has a bad reputation because he wished to stop Italian vineyards being extended; he therefore decreed that many vineyards within the Roman Empire should be uprooted. This was so as to encourage the cultivation of grain within the Roman Empire. It may be doubted as to whether the wily peasant growers actually did up-root their vineyards – within various wine regions the vine was still being cultivated,

An aureus showing the likeness of Domitian, first century AD. (*Private collection/ Bridgeman Art Library*)

and the decree was later rescinded by the Emperor Probus.

COLUMELLA'S *RE RUSTICA*

Lucius Junius Moderatus Columella seems to have done his major work in the middle of the first century AD. Columella may have been born in southern Spain, but he later went to Italy and wrote about many things concerning trees. His *Re Rustica* includes important and still relevant comments on the cultivation of the vine in all its aspects, including pruning, grafting and general care. Even if one cannot tackle the Latin, Columella is worth reading because he wrote about the vines and wines of Italy, which those who read him were able to find of use and turn to their profit.

INDIAN WINE

It may astonish many to learn that wine has apparently been known in India for thousands of years. Alexander the Great, who invaded this part of the continent, is said to have propagated the vine and the well-known 'Rubaiyat' of the Persian poet, Omar Khayyam (1048–1131) wrote enthusiastically about wine. Various emperors, including Shah Jahem who built the Taj Mahal may, it is suggested, have tried the wines of the royal vineyards in the Maharashtra, but there are no accounts of these wines although one emperor is shown on a gold coin brandishing a wine cup.

In 1884, at the Great Calcutta Exhibition, some Indian wines were on show but, almost immediately afterwards, the phylloxera struck the Indian vineyards, like those of Europe. So it was not until the end of the twentieth century that Mr Sham Chougoule, chairman of the Indago Group of Companies, who had visited France and developed a love of wines, began to plan to produce wine in India.

His vineyards were carefully selected on the upper slopes of the Sahandri mountains, French authorities being brought in to advise from Rheims and special cuttings of Chardonnay, Ugni Blanc and Pinot Blanc were also imported, together with a complete plant and all the tanks, bottles, corks and requirements for the production of a sparkling wine. Even the wine maker came from a famous Champagne establishment. The cost of the operation was gigantic, as may be supposed.

The sparkling wine was first shown at an international exhibition, to the astonishment of those who sampled it and, as may be imagines, to the amazement of the Champenois. Of course, the use of the term

'Champagne' was strictly forbidden in Europe, but the first sparkling wine seems to have been successful in India and another plant was later established near the first one. What sort of overall success there may be with this truly innovative wine is uncertain but it is of major interest that it has been attempted.

WINE, WORMWOOD AND VERMOUTH

Many producers will state, proudly, that their wines have been known and popular for many years, many centuries. Grapes, certainly, have always been a valued crop, whether or not they made wine, because their sugar content appealed to people who knew sweetened foods as luxuries. The black teeth of Elizabeth I were virtually a status symbol – she could eat all the sweetmeats she wanted. Yet, around the Mediterranean, cradle of many wines, it wasn't always possible to make wine sweet enough to appeal for drinking. Vinegar, useful but not endlessly so, has its limitations in the kitchen. So what happened to many of the wines that didn't quite succeed as pleasant drinks – often from mountain vineyards where the sun didn't ripen the grapes as it might or those that resulted from bad wine making or keeping which turned a possible commercial beverage into something definitely different from a table wine?

Hippocrates, Father of Medicine (*c.* 400–375 BC), came of a family well-known for being adept physicians and surgeons. They had certainly known the use of herbs, barks, flowers, fruits, and spices to enhance wines, but, in addition, such drinks acquired medicinal properties that were known and appreciated. These additives were known throughout all the first medical schools, but one ingredient tends to recur: *artemisia absinthium*, a name which, in German (from which so many languages derive) became known as 'wormwood' or '*vermut*'.

Drinks of a slightly bitter character didn't necessarily come into the nursery category of 'It will do you good because it's nasty', but it is obvious that a tinge of bitterness can perk up a jaded palate. (It is not to be assumed that any bitterness will prove to be aphrodisiac, although many buyers of 'bitters' suppose them to be so.)

Vermouth is a wine. It starts as such and should be

Hippocrates, Father of Medicine. (*Museo Archeologico Nazionale, Naples/ Bridgeman Art Library*)

treated as such; old bottles of vermouth, left over from last Christmas, may be terrible if used in mixes. The use of various herbs, spices and other ingredients varied the wine and the first commercially made vermouth was produced in Turin, north Italy, in the eighteenth century. Other firms, such as some that were confronted with the over-production of wines that couldn't be easily acceptable as table wines into the market (Marseilles and, later, Chambéry), became the great vermouth centres, as they are today.

Until quite recently many assumed that 'Italian' vermouth was sweet or sweetish, 'French' dry. In fact the great vermouth establishments make a range of both sweet and dry vermouths, each house having its own recipes and style. Chambéry vermouth is rather different, being traditionally drunk by itself, not as part of a 'mix' or cocktail.

The important thing to realise about vermouth is that, like other wines, it will deteriorate if left open indefinitely. Two or three days for a bottle, stoppered and kept in the refrigerator, may keep it adequately fresh, but after that. . . .

Travellers should make use of the local vermouths around the Mediterranean – Cretans, for example, are proud of the way the herb dittany brought them customers from many markets to use this herb. It is also useful to realise that the categories of vermouth within countries can vary: one place's 'dry' may be definitely sweetish, whereas a 'sweet' vermouth may be less sweet than the visitor expects. In the New World methods of wine-making have enabled wine to be used and enjoyed without making much vermouth, but the huge vermouth firms elsewhere enable it to be supplied with such vermouths as they may wish for their cocktails.

KYLIX, CUPS AND CHALICES

Considering that so many drinking vessels are made of fragile material – pottery, glass, porcelain – it is astonishing that so many have survived intact. The kylix, a shallow two-handled cup, was used in ancient times by both Greeks and Romans. The idea of reclining on a couch while being served seems odd to us today, but the kylix was certainly easy to pass from one drinker to another and slaves would have seen that adequate amounts of liquid were put into each kylix. Jugs for replenishing drinking cups were part of an attendant's basic equipment. As wine was seldom served undiluted with herbs, spices and other additives – it might have been both unpleasant and sometimes very sour and sharp if it had been – attendants who brought up wine from the store or

A woman fills various vessels with wine in a depiction taken from the *Speculum humanae Salvationis*. (© *The British Library/ Heritage-Images*)

cellar would have sampled it before they served it. St Augustine's mother, Saint Monica, who used to be sent down to the cellar in her parents' house to fetch up any wine required, unashamedly dabbled her fingers in the 'uncut' wine, from which the family tagged her with the name 'Meribibula', because she obviously enjoyed the taste.

Formal wine cups, such as might be offered to the guest of honour, both in these ancient times and through the medieval period, are often ornate and, holding a fair amount of liquid, the fact that they have two handles is a safeguard for those who pass them at table. Often these drinking vessels, which were used in rituals before Christianity, to signify that the 'shared cup' was a sign of fellowship, have covers. Much discussion has arisen about this but I think it is most likely to be practical: if a cup were covered then, without the cover being removed, no poison or sinister substance could be put in without notice being taken. And, when such formal functions took place in large halls, where birds might fly in and out, there was a practical need to keep the drink shielded from droppings.

Cups or chalices used in religious rituals could not be at risk if exposed once their contents had been hallowed or consecrated. It would rest on the officiating minister to shield the consecrated liquid, by covering it, but the need to do so of course, depended on whether the congregation, in Christian times, partook of 'both kinds' – wine as well as bread – which priests would do, and in later times on whether it was a Reformed establishment or not.

One thing that may not be known to those who admire the wonderful chalices and altar vessels seen in museums and often used today, is that, even though devout persons presented gold vessels for the glorification of God, it is still usually silver that is in use. That is because silver, from very ancient times, has been found to be less of a conveyor of infection than gold – gold is a softer metal.

And one tiny survival: in early times, the most precious drops of a wine would be poured out to the gods – as, in the Old Testament, David pours out the water he has craved for from a particular well, and when some of his men have gone through the enemy lines to get it, David pours it upon the ground – because it represents the blood of those who sought it. And still. . . . Years ago, before bottling lines were routine in modern wineries, and one was taught to bottle wines by hand, when, having left the wine from the cask to fill the bottle, the level of the wine came up to the point at which the cork might be put in, the bottle would be picked up and flicked, so that the very last drops of the wine might be scattered upon the ground. Then one would stopper the bottle. The flick of wine on the cellar floor or, out in the country, on the ground, was a survival of the old, old 'libation', a thanksgiving to those who had given their sweat to achieve the wine.

MEDIEVAL WINE ORDERS

In former times those engaged in crafts, trades and other specialised activities in Europe often formed associations: such societies might not only regulate professional activities, but would achieve charitable purposes and help members fallen on hard times. Although some of these 'wine orders' ceased to function actively as time went on, many remained doing the same work and, certainly in the period of depression between the two World Wars, some were revived or, even, started up. The picturesque robes, the ceremonies and feasts of such wine orders is good to see and can promote business. Membership, given to those who have served the cause of the particular wine, is a privilege, although it should be noted that membership of such a wine fraternity does not always imply that the member is an authority on that particular wine.

It is only possible to mention some of the more ancient and well-known wine orders, but a complete list is given, with their history, in *Le Grand Livre des Confréries des Vins de France* (1971):

Antica Confraria de Saint-Andiu de la Galiniera (Hérault and Biterrois), 1140
Jurade de Saint Emilion, 1199
Commande Majeure de Roussillon pour garder Le Devoir de la Vigne et du Vin, 1374
Confrérie Saint Etienne (Alsace), established in the fifteenth century
Ordre Illustre des Chevaliers de Méduse (Côtes de Provence), 1690
Confrérie des Chevaliers du Sacavin (Angers), 1904
Confrérie des Chevaliers du Tastevin, 1934
Confrérie des Chevaliers de la Chante Pleure (Vouvray), 1937

Compagnons du Beaujolais, 1947

Ordre des Chevaliers Bretvins (Nantes), 1948

Commanderie du Bontemps de Médoc et des Graves, 1949

Ordre des Coteaux de Champagne, 1956

Les Chevaliers de Sancerre, 1964

Some of the orders are also associated with the spirits of their region and even with cheese!

WINESKINS AND TRAVELLERS' CUPS

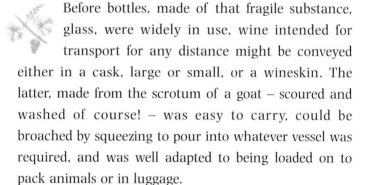 Before bottles, made of that fragile substance, glass, were widely in use, wine intended for transport for any distance might be conveyed either in a cask, large or small, or a wineskin. The latter, made from the scrotum of a goat – scoured and washed of course! – was easy to carry, could be broached by squeezing to pour into whatever vessel was required, and was well adapted to being loaded on to pack animals or in luggage.

Cups were of course in use since the earliest times for drinking, but travellers needed something less fragile. Bone was used and it's possible that those who ventured to the northern areas of Europe made use of horn, not the huge drinking horns of Viking feasts, but smaller vessels carved from the horns of domestic animals. Soldiers had some access to metal and,

Men carrying wine from the vineyards in the ravine of the Ribeiro dos Soccoridos

certainly in the Roman army, they needed to be able to carry a cup with them because it might not always be possible to scoop up enough water from a pool or pond when on a route march.

THE BUZZ AND THE BUMPER

A buzz – originally spelt 'buz', as in Thomas Love Peacock's novel *Gryll Grange* (1860) – occurs when the last of the wine in a bottle or decanter fills the glass of the person to be served, or who, with port, is serving himself (or, I suppose, herself), so that the wine not only fills but bulges over the surface of the glass. Originally, as my dear friend the late Warner Allen stated, a wager was involved: the person who said a 'buzz' was likely, poured out the wine and, proving their point, was given a bottle for everyone around the table. Today, when the custom seems to be more applicable to port, the person who achieves a buzz merely gets a generous helping of the next bottle.

It has been said that this custom still exists in some colleges that are proud of their wines, but one fears that, these days, when many learned establishments have sold off the contents of their cellars, it may only be a legend.

Bumper is a term that seems to have originated in the seventeenth century. It means a glass filled to the brim, which does not necessarily imply that the wine was of good quality. It seems to have come into use among those who were drinking heavily, and was much associated with riotous young men drinking regardless. It should be remembered that if a toast or a wish for health and success were associated with some person or cause, then the company would be expected to 'honour' or signify the thorough endorsement of the theme by drinking deeply, possibly with 'no heeltaps'.

TWO

THE BRITISH INFLUENCE

THE FIRST ENGLISH WINE WRITER?

Because wine encourages conversation there must have been many comments written down about it since it was first made. Classical scholars can cite many instances of what the great writers of the past wrote about what they drank, but in England, for obvious reasons, not much is recorded. One, however, who did set down his love of wine was the Yorkshireman, Alcuin (*c.* 735–804). He was librarian and master of the York schools until he was called by the Emperor Charlemagne to go and teach at the Emperor's court. His writings, cited by Helen Waddell in her books *The Wandering Scholars* (1932) and *Mediaeval Latin Lyrics* (1929), indicate how, when he had to return to England, he missed French wines. To a friend he writes, 'The wine is gone from our wineskins and bitter beer rageth in our bellies.' And he mentions that another friend has promised him two cases of wine and gives instructions for its safe carriage. His songs urging the cuckoo to return and revive spring are certainly the wishes of anyone longing for easier, happier seasons.

GEOFFREY CHAUCER, THE GREAT ENGLISH TELLER OF TALES

Geoffrey Chaucer (*c.* 1344–1400) was certainly a man of wine. Both his father and grandfather were members of the Vintners' Company and,

Geoffrey Chaucer (*c.* 1344–1400), the son and grandson of a vintner.
(*Private collection/Bridgeman Art Library*)

although young Geoffrey didn't go into the wine trade, he became quite influential in various posts. He married Philippa Swynford, the sister-in-law of John of Gaunt, the Duke of Lancaster, the most powerful man in England. Chaucer became Controller of the Customs and, also, Clerk of the King's Works; he was influential and probably thought no more of going out to France, where he had been a prisoner in the Reims campaign – than we should think of going to the Isle of Wight.

All wine references in Chaucer's works are pertinent but there is one that gives an awful warning about the produce of hot country vineyards, where the strength of the wines might rise and be suddenly disastrous to drinkers. Julian Jeffs, who has made a special study of sherry, and the wines of this region, is uncertain about the 'wyn of Lepe' by Chaucer, but the reference is irresistible, especially if one can read it in the original 'Pardoner's Tale':

Now kepe yow fro the white and fro the rede
And namely from the white wyn of Lepe,
That is to sell in Fysshstrete or in Chepe
This wyn of Spaigne crepeth subtilly

In othere wynes, growynge faste by,
Of which there ryseth swich fumositee
That whan a man hath dronken draughtes thre,
And weneth that he be at hoom in Chepe
He is in Spaigne, right at the toune of Lepe,
Nat at the Rochele, ne at Burdeux toun.

Hot country wines may indeed be higher in alcohol than those of cooler vineyards. If only Chaucer could have kept a tasting book!

'Fysshe' is Fish Street in the heart of the City of London and 'Chepe' is Cheapside. Whether Chaucer went to La Rochelle, where the local wines were, at his time, plentiful, is not known, but he may well have gone to Bordeaux because of the wine trade.

THE VINTNERS' COMPANY

The great halls, property of the various livery companies in the City of London, are very varied: some are ancient, some modern – rebuilt after being bombed in World War II – but most have

The installation process of HRH The Duke of Gloucester as Master of the Vintners' Company in 1953. The Duke, in the centre, is shown with the Company's Wine Porters with the beadle and swan marker. (*The Vintners' Company*)

treasures relating to the activities of members throughout the ages.

The Vintners' Company ranks eleventh in the precedence of City companies and received its first charter in 1364; this was in fact a grant of monopoly for trade with Gascony which included duties of search throughout England and the right to sell herrings and cloths to the Gascons. Members of the Livery (the Company) gave generously to the Company and, although their influence declined over the centuries, their charitable works – many undertaken by the widows and families of members – enabled them to retain, even today, certain powers, including, for freemen by patrimony or servitude, 'the privilege of selling wine without licence in London within three miles of its walls and in certain specified ports and thoroughfare towns between London and Dover and London and Berwick'.

Engraving by R. Acon of a drawing of Vintners' Hall by T.H. Shepherd, c. 1828. (*The Vintners' Company*)

However, the turbulent times of subsequent centuries presented many problems and, in the Commonwealth period, it suffered because of its adherence to Charles I. The Restoration of the Stuarts did not see a revival of its fortunes, and the Great Fire of London in 1666 destroyed the original Hall and damaged many properties nearby – this, remember, was before fire insurance. Under William and Mary the privileges taken away by James II were restored, but the Vintners couldn't recover their previous power. Their estates, however, and the charities they directed, increased in value.

After the fire, the Hall was rebuilt on the same grounds, though on a somewhat smaller scale. There are many things of great interest in the Hall and adjacent buildings today and anyone able to visit the Hall and its environs should allow at least an hour to see the works of art and pictures. The display of medallions in the entrance hall is well worth looking at and the displays of plate and the portraits all merit study. The windows should also be inspected, a modern one showing different grape varieties and St Martin, patron saint of the Company.

The building is not, however, as some erroneously suppose, the former house of the then Lord Mayor of London, although Sir Henry Picard did live nearby and a plaque in the Hall commemorates how he feasted

'Five Kings' there. It is fair to say, though, that the King of Cyprus, who was included, was apparently going round Europe trying to borrow funds, not truly a 'King' like the others. But all this is still debated. What isn't, however, is the antiquity of the Company's records, the first deed for the Hall being witnessed, among others, by Geoffrey Chaucer's father, John. The Vintners are proud of their hospitable traditions, having entertained the four sons of Queen Victoria and the four sons of King George V. In addition to its charitable activities, the Vintners' Company today organises a considerable education programme, lectures in London and in some major British towns and cities. It also arranges courses for students in many other countries, and runs a quite luxurious assembly of bungalows in a suburb of Eastbourne, where a number of elderly people are able to live and, at need, be cared for.

The Vintners have owned swans on the Thames since before records were kept, which is why they feature on their arms. In former times the swan, of course, was a game bird, of some substance. The birds are carefully tended – the first record is for their care in the great frost of 1522 – and they are marked, indicating to whom they belong. The Vintners' swans bear two 'nicks' on the beak of each bird – done very carefully so as to avoid suffering – while those belonging to the Dyers' Company have only one nick. The remaining swans belong to the Crown. The 'two nicks' which used to denote the Vintners' swans, became distorted into 'two necks', a sign of various pubs. Each July the swans are 'upped' or taken from the Thames to be counted and ringed.

There is a 'Swan Feast' given by the vintners every November, but sometimes the numbers of the birds – assailed by the influx of Canada Geese – can give cause for alarm. Yet swan, properly cooked, can apparently be pleasant, although it seems as if it may be some-what 'gamey'. Indeed, in the Middle Ages Dr Andrew Boorde, who seems to have had some experience of various exotic fare, wrote that 'Old swans be very difficult of digestion.'

The festivals of many of the wine fraternities usually coincide with the main wine seasons: vintage, flower-ing, plus summer and immediately prior to Christmas.

QUEEN ELEANOR AND THE ORIGIN OF 'CLARET'

For 299 years the English crown owned a swathe of France that extended from the River Loire to the Pyrenees. Aquitaine – the 'land of waters' – was ruled by a series of dominating dukes, one of whom was a writer of charming verses; the

Effigy of Eleanor of Aquitaine (*c.* 1122–1204), Queen of France, then of England, at Fontevrault Abbey, France. (*Fontevrault Abbey, France/Bridgeman Art Library*)

duchy was both powerful and influential. But in the twelfth century the Duke had no son, only two daughters and, as this Duke wanted to go off on a pilgrimage to Compostella, the elder daughter, Eleanor, was betrothed to the son of the then King of France, so that her lands might be secured. Eleanor is one of the mysterious great ladies of the Middle Ages: even when she was in her mid-thirties a poet wrote, not necessarily just to flatter,

> Were the whole world mine
> From the sea to the Rhine –
> I'd give it all if the Queen of
>   England lay in my arms.

Eleanor, who always ruled her own lands, became Queen of France while actually on her wedding journey. But Prince Louis, now King, wished to go on a crusade. Eleanor – who later said of him, 'I thought to have married a man, not a monk' – went along as well and there are delightful legends about her en route.

Once back in France even the Pope couldn't reconcile the two, and dissolution of the marriage was achieved, although poor old Louis had to get through two wives yet before he achieved a son. Eleanor, having noticed the young Henry of Anjou, decided he was a likely husband for her. This was the man who carried, like his father, a spring of broom in his hat or helmet – *planta genista*. In 1154 Henry and Eleanor became King and Queen of England.

Eleanor, who was the sort of woman who made history, is always garlanded with charm. It was at this time that the wines produced in the Bordeaux region – mostly in the Graves area then – were differentiated from those coming in from the 'high country', the darker, fruitier products of further afield. These had to contend with the lighter, '*plus clair*' wines of the Bordeaux region. So export markets liked and asked for the '*plus clair*' wines, which became known as 'clairet'. Even when the English were expelled from Bordeaux, the wine trade remained brisk between the two countries, and up to 1803 the British Royal

Standard is recorded as bearing the fleur de lys of France.

So – the *'plus clair'* wine remained a favourite of the English. The rest of the world heads certain sections of the wine list as 'red Bordeaux', but the British use the term 'claret'. Attempts have been made to get them to fall into line with everyone else and at one time a few years ago the then representative of the Wine and Spirit Association of Great Britain was asked to justify this individuality before the pundits of the Common Market at Brussels. Fortunately, this man was not only eminently respected and experienced in the wine trade, he was married to a delicious French lady; so, while the common marketeers posed their questions and had to wait for these to be translated for the benefit of the supposedly semi-educated British, the English-man was able calmly to consider what replies he should make. Eventually, when asked why an exception should be made for the United Kingdom, he carefully phrased his reply to the effect that, after all, an exception should be made in this instance – because hadn't the English crown owned the slice of France that then included the Bordeaux region for 299 years? Well, then! And so the British and those throughout the English-speaking world – still call red Bordeaux claret.

It should be noted that today there is a wine 'clairet', which is reddish-pink, but rather more 'important' than a rosé. It is subject to regulations and can make a delicious drink.

PONTAC IN LONDON

The word 'Pontac' occurs in many accounts of wines of the seventeenth and eighteenth centuries in London. It was, in fact, the family name of winemakers established, according to my colleague Clive Coates MW, since the fifteenth century. The Pontac family owned a fine house in Bordeaux itself, plus an increasing number of estates, including Haut Brion. The Pontacs of the late sixteenth century owned ships and rose to eminence in Bordeaux in many ways. It was in 1666 that Arnaud de Pontac sent his son François-Auguste to London, where, immediately after the Great Fire of London, business became brisk. François-August opened a tavern 'The Sign of Pontac's Head' and, for some time to come the wine, whether it was that of Haut Brion or not, seems to have been called 'Pontac'.

Among those who were enthusiastic about Pontac were John Dryden, Daniel Defoe, Jonathan Swift and John Evelyn; 'Pontack's', as a chic eating place for gentlemen, is referred to in Congreve's *Love for Love* (1685). In 1705 the *London Gazette* lists 'Pontack Prize-

Wines' and, a little later, '200 hogsheads of New Pontac'. This must be one of the earliest instances of a shipper's wines enjoying the reputation of wines from specific estates.

What Pontac was like we shall probably never know, although white wines as well as red seem to have been shipped. The latter probably came from the family's estates in Blanquefort, but the Pontacs had properties in the Entre-Deux-Mers, at Podensac and, also at this early date when the Graves region remained 'the cradle of claret', as far up the Médoc as Pez and St Estèphe, as well as Haut Brion. It is, of course, likely that many of those who merely ordered 'Pontac' supposed themselves to be drinking some form of Haut Brion, but in 1723 the English merchant who had charge of the cellars of the then Prince of Wales – later George II – listed the wines of 'La Tour, Lafite, Château Margaux and Pontac', naming Pontac as if it were an estate or the level of those other illustrious properties.

SIR WALTER RALEIGH'S VINE?

 Grapes were plentiful in North Carolina as early as 1524, according to the Florentines who explored it. In 1584, according to one of the

Sir Walter Raleigh (*c.* 1554–1618). (*Private collection/Bridgeman Art Library*)

many tales of North American vines and wines given in *The Wines of America* by Leon D. Adams (1984), Sir Walter Raleigh sent two colleagues to explore, who reported that, as regards grapes, 'the like abundance is not to be found'. Indeed, Raleigh is credited with discovering the Scuppernong grape on Roanoke Island and for many years this vine was credited with his name; there is a famous 'Mother vine' on the island, which is said to be about three centuries old – and is still yielding grapes.

ROMAN VINES AND ENGLISH PIONEERS

The Romans seem to have introduced the grape vine to England – probably the Pinot Noir – and villas and towns had vineyards and made wine. The Roman army were issued with drinking cups as part of their basic equipment, and had a wine ration; the centurion's badge of office was a vine staff. There appears to have been a period of about two hundred years of mild climate, and excavations of villas and settlements often show terracing and even cellars, indicating that vines were grown and wine made. Vines and grapes also feature on many carvings and stones. This is noted in Hugh Barty-King's superb book *A Tradition of English Wine* (1977). Unfortunately, there seems to have been a climate change when the Gulf Stream altered its course in about 1350 and, although monastic establishments, needing wine for sacramental purposes, continued to have vineyards, the acquisition of the south-west of France by the English crown for 299 years made it easy to bring in wine from there.

Whatever occurred with the climate, the coming of Christianity to Britain had made it essential for religious establishments to plant and maintain their own vineyards. The great monasteries were often self-sufficient, providing food and drink, medical skills and nursing to those who came to them, in addition to their spiritual activities. The stillrooms and libraries of many monasteries could be a valuable source of medical lore and treatment as well as of learning. The hospices of the great establishments, such as the Hospices de Beaune, are also wonderful as works of art.

In Domesday Book there are over forty vineyards listed and there may have been more. These include vineyards in Kensington, Staines, Westminster and Holborn. Many street and place names still mention vines, indicating that the tradition was maintained. The Dissolution of the Monasteries by Henry VIII did not wholly destroy many vineyards, although this period did coincide with what became known as 'the little Ice Age' of bad weather. Vineyards were still cultivated and vines were grown under glass in later centuries.

'The noblemen of Elizabethan England were proud to fill their cellars not only with Rhenish and Gascon wine but with the fresh wine of the country', Hugh Barty-King states. And he cites Shakespeare's lines in *Henry VIII*, given to Cranmer, who had known the vines of Westwell Priory in Kent, given to him by Henry VIII:

> In her days every man shall eat in safety
> Under his own vine what he plants.
> It is a long tradition in England and Wales.

At Hatfield House, Lord Salisbury planted 30,000 French vines. In 1666 *The English Vineyard Vindicated*, a book with a preface by John Evelyn, appeared but although vineyards continued to be laid down, the way in which the wines were made is insufficiently recorded.

In the nineteenth century Lord Bute established a vineyard at Castell Coch, north of Cardiff, although again the press at Cardiff Castle has never been definitely established. In fact, there remain numerous shreds and relics of the festoons of vineyards that used to proliferate over Victorian porches and trellises alongside the country houses. These were probably ornamental, but a nasty plague was about to attack them – first, downy mildew, then phylloxera (see entries). It was only after World War II that vineyards began to be planted again in England and Wales. The skill of growers and makers has astonished those who thought wine could never be made in England or Wales. The pioneers of English vineyards in the immediate postwar period were of great importance and the research and devoted work of many in England and in Wales resulted in the English Vineyards Association being formed in 1967. There are now numerous vineyards in England and Wales making wine, and their annual functions are impressive, although unfortunately no state aid is given by the British Government to makers. All types of wine are made, including sparkling and red. It is not a product that needs an apology. The knowledge and professionalism of English and Welsh wine makers has impressed many through the wine world. Of course the wines are not 'the same as' certain famous names. They can, though, be very enjoyable.

A PORTUGUESE WINE AND AN ENGLISH TRADITION

Many would suppose that the alliance between England and Portugal was established in 1703, when the Methuen Treaty gave certain fiscal advantages to Portuguese wines in Britain. But the two sea-going nations, England and Portugal, had already pledged perpetual friendship by the Treaty of Windsor in 1386. In *Portugal's Wines and Wine-makers* (1992) Richard Mayson stresses that 'By the end of the fifteenth century Lisbon was one of the world's great trading centres. The empire building that followed the epic voyages of Prince Henry the Navigator, Gil Eanes, Bartolomeu Dias and Vasco da Gama put Portugal on the map and expanded her trading network to include Africa, India and Brazil.' Prince Henry the Navigator didn't go on the great voyages he inspired but anyone who has travelled out to Sagres, from which he would look westwards across the Atlantic, can understand his wish to go further. For, it shouldn't be forgotten, Prince Henry was half-English, his mother being the daughter of John of Gaunt, Duke of Lancaster. From this time the English were trading wool for salt cod with the Portuguese and possibly had been doing so earlier. Salted fish were valuable provisions for anyone going exploring.

King William III and Queen Mary, engraving by Robert White after an unknown artist. (*By courtesy of the National Portrait Gallery, London*)

It was because of this long friendship that when King William and Queen Mary came to the English throne in the Glorious Revolution of 1688, those who wished to drink to their new sovereign had a problem. King William was a Dutchman – could they drink the toast to a sovereign in gin, the liquor that gave the world the expression 'Dutch courage' from the sixteenth-century wars against the Spaniards? The incoming King and Queen didn't seem to have any obvious association with any one wine, until those with long memories of wines nudged the royal butlers and caterers into remembering Portugal. . . . Of course! Trade in the Portuguese wines that appealed greatly to the British and north European markets was starting. Christiano Kopke began in business in 1638, Warre in 1670.

Wine made by this method appealed enormously to the northern markets, so that this style of wine increased and King William III having slapped a tax on French wines at the time, the advantages of drinking Portuguese wines were obvious. 'Dutch Billy' wasn't wholly popular with the British but, although it is not dated, the British then began to drink to the monarch in possession – and, for the reasons of cheapness and availability, they usually drank a Portuguese wine. Under Queen Anne and the Hanoverian Georges the court ceased to be chic, but those who preferred the moderate stability of the monarch in preference to the sovereigns 'over the water' went on drinking red wines, often from Portugal.

So, although it is not definite as to when the toast to the sovereign began to be honoured by being drunk in port, it has been so for a very long time.

FORTIFIED WINES AND WARFARE

XERES, OR SHERRY

 If you pronounce the beginning of this word as a 'sh' you will understand why the name of sherry became what it is today. There have been many discussions about this word, some authorities supposing Falstaff's euology of 'sack' to refer to sherry, others averring that 'sherris sack' merely means a wine intended for export, the word 'sec' establishing the dry style of wine. Or there is the theory that 'sec' is short for 'sacco' – to take out, therefore, a wine for exporting.

This is the wine that stems from southern Spain, but at least since the time of Queen Elizabeth I Britons have enjoyed a version of it. The sherry vineyards are on white soil called *albariza*, and several grapes are utilised – the Listan or Palomino Blanco notably for the great sweet wines.

It is important to sort out the various types of sherry, but the one of great importance is the fino, on the surface of which is a curious substance, known as 'flor' appears. This flor sometimes covers the surface of the wine in the cask, sometimes seems only to be evident as a tiny iridescence on the surface. The importance of flor is that the wine made in a butt where it has formed will be a fino, others, lacking flor, will be oloroso – often very good wines but not the same.

One important thing to note is that all sherry ferments right out, any sweetening that may be required – as for some of the popular blends in northern markets – will have been separately added.

The Solera System
This is a special type of wine store. All the wines in the butts contained within it are, as it were, like a family. When they are drawn off, the butts are 'refreshed' with a similar sort of wine from the same solera. The matter is complex and anyone seriously interested should consult one of the several authoritative books on the subject.

Ageing
Sherry does not bear a vintage date, although some historic sherry establishments may put when the house was founded on their labels. There is no point in laying down a sherry; indeed, if it happens to be a dry wine, it may deteriorate after a time. Sweeter sherries can sometimes last and be drinkable for years.

Styles of Sherry
Fino is a very dry, crisp young wine. People who set aside some of the remains of the bottle for future drinking are likely to give the next guests a nasty experience; if a bottle cannot be finished, put it in the

refrigerator or decant it into a half bottle. Aeration will cause it to go soggy and dreary.

Amontillado is a matured fino, and can be a beautiful drink. In the Jerez region people may prefer to drink an amontillado as an apéritif during the day, but fino before dinner. Both should be lightly chilled.

Oloroso is a fragrant and darkish-toned wine, which certainly need not be a sweet wine. Manzanilla is a specially delicate fino; it can only be matured at the coast – at Sanlucar de Barrameda – and it is supposed to acquire a type of salty tang from the proximity of the sea. If it is moved to Jerez it becomes an ordinary fino.

Palo Cortado is a curious, rather rare sherry, darkish in tone but very dry.

Other 'Sherries'

Sherry can come only from Spain, but many other countries make a lightly fortified wine according to the sherry procedure. A vast range of quality is available and no wine lover should eschew trying one of the wines that may term themselves 'sherry' in other countries. Many can be very good, most should be of interest.

Blending

According to the market in which a sherry is to be sold, it may be blended to appeal to that public. In

Ripe Palomino Fino grapes on vines growing in the Jerez region. (*Mick Rock/Cephas*)

northern countries there is a natural preference for wines that are slightly softer, even sweeter. After all, wine is a commercial commodity! And 'For the UK, call it dry but make it sweet' is a saying established for many years. A public not likely to drink fine or even much wine with a meal may opt for a sweetish apéritif, whereas someone in a dry, hot climate may prefer something crisp and likely to perk up the palate. Many sherries sold and publicised as 'dry' are in fact 'helped' by the addition of plumper wines until they are hardly the palate-scraping dry wines that might be found in the region. There is also the fact that in the northern export markets certain sherries are definitely luscious – some can be delectable, but they are not often meant to be drunk as table wines.

One thing that is true, however, is that in the sherry region in southern Spain, sherry is drunk with meals as well as providing an apéritif. There are many agreeable pairings of dry or dryish sherry with foods, notably the 'tapas' or snacks that proliferate in southern Spain. Fish, olives, minute salads, vegetables with dips that may be slightly piquant or unctuous, slivers of smoked meat are all pleasant with many sorts of sherry.

MARSALA

This is a fortified wine, made in the south of Sicily and first evolved, in its present state, by John Woodhouse of Liverpool, who began to export it in 1773. It enjoyed a great vogue and there's an interesting order from Lord Nelson, then trying to write with his left hand, ordering Marsala for the Mediterranean fleet. Today, though, the taste for this wine is mainly restricted to Italian eating places; the wine, fullish in style, only comes to the notice of many Britons when it is used to make sweet dishes, although dry Marsala is suitable to serve like dry Madeira or white port.

The Marsala establishments, nowadays under the control of Florio, which belongs to Cinzano, are impressive – but unfortunately the original owners didn't live in them but preferred the pleasures of Paris and other cities. The beauty of Sicily, however, is something no wine enthusiast should miss if it is possible to visit the beautiful palaces and the variations on Marsala *in situ* it can be fascinating.

PORT

 Port is one of the great fortified wines of the world, very much a wine created for the British taste and, in certain instances, seen at the peak of its perfection in the UK. It is made in a defined area of the upper Douro, in northern Portugal, from a variety of grapes, both red and white. The grapes, traditionally pressed by foot in a stone trough called a **lagar**, are now often mechanically pressed; or an 'autovinificator' is used, which achieves the same end. At a certain point in the fermentation the process is arrested by the addition of brandy. The wine, once made, then goes down the River Douro to Oporto or, more correctly to Vila Nova de Gaia, where the port shippers have their lodges or establishments. Here it is sorted out, differentiated according to quality and the style of wine for which it is destined.

Although the majority of ports are destined to spend their life in wood or cask (the pipe) the youngish wines can be bottled early and sold as 'Ruby Port', the colour being as the name implies. A fine ruby, left to mature in wood, will lighten in colour and increase in delicacy and may become a Fine Old Tawny Port. The best of the tawnies are as fine as any fortified wine – and the sort of wine the shippers drink themselves for sheer pleasure. Inexpensive tawnies may be made by blending ruby and white port. White port is used as an apéritif; it is made from white grapes only and is a pleasant warm weather drink. The finer white ports are completely dry, the fermentation process being allowed to finish using the grape sugar before the brandy is added. Cheaper white ports can be sweet or slightly sweet.

(People are often confused about the sort of wine that port is – but all port is a fortified wine and therefore of higher strength than table wine. All port, because its fermentation has been arrested by the addition of brandy, is possessed of a certain sweetness – but this should be a subtle thing, never cloying, and the wine should be balanced. The ports of each port house will differ in style; vintage ports differ in both according to the style of the house that 'declares' them and their vintage.)

Obviously, each establishment making port will follow its own 'house style'. Until fairly recently, the UK market was slightly aloof from that of the wines produced by the Portuguese port houses. The differences remain but the friendship between many establishments are firm. The situation is slightly complicated by the fact that many wine countries make fortified wines that, outside the EC, they call 'port', but which are simply not the same as the wines that come from the Upper Douro, are matured in the 'lodges' at Vila Nova de Gaia and then go for export. (It is also interesting that wines kept up the Douro develop in a slightly different way.) In many New World countries there are first-rate fortified wines, but they may only be called 'port' in their homelands; one infuriated North American produced a wine which he registered as 'Starboard'. So, for the time being and until there is an international board dealing with the names of wines, 'Port comes only from Portugal'.

Vintage Port

Some consider this to be the greatest dessert wine in the world. It is the wine made from the ports of one single year – which has been 'declared' as a vintage by the shipper whose wine it is. It is up to the shipper to decide whether to declare a vintage or not, and although certain years are declared by many port houses, by no means everyone declares the same years. Each vintage year, naturally, has its own individuality. The wine selected as a vintage is bottled after spending only two or three years in wood. In former times it was invariably shipped to the UK and bottled there, but vintage ports must nowadays be bottled in Portugal. In former times it might be handled and bottled by a number of merchants buying it, as well as by the shipper in his premises in the UK.

The port in bottles is then laid down to mature, a

splash on the side of the bottle indicating where its first recumbent position has been. This is important because the formation of the crust must be allowed to develop gradually for the first 5 or 6 years of the port's life. If the bottle is disturbed at this point, the crust never seems to form satisfactorily and the deposit may remain in suspension in the wine, making it unpleasant to drink and spoiling the beautiful colour. Vintage port, even in a light year, is not really ready to drink before it is 8 to 10 years old, and ideally not before it is 15 years from its vintage. It can live very much longer than that – ports a century old are still sometimes shown to privileged guests of the port trade. If vintage port has to be moved, it will reform its crust quite satisfactorily, after a certain number of weeks or months, if this has originally formed properly. However, it lives on this crust and should always be carefully decanted off before it is served.

As the port bottle is specially designed to enable the wine to be laid down for a long while – with a long, slightly bulging neck, into which a long, high quality cork is inserted – it should be handled with especial care. Because the extraction of a cork can present difficulty after many years and it may crumble, the neck of the bottle is sometimes taken off. Vintage port should be drunk within 24 hours of being decanted as it will fade with exposure to the atmosphere. But ruby, tawny and white ports (the last should be chilled) may be served for up to a week after the bottle is opened, or after they have been decanted to show off their colour: there is no deposit.

Vintage Character Port

A wine of particular quality, blended, and ready for drinking once it has been bottled. It has great appeal, especially in circumstances where people want to drink a fine port but cannot consume a whole bottle – or cannot afford a vintage.

Late Bottled Vintage Port

Port of a single year which has been matured in wood for 3 to 6 years – unlike the 2 to 3 of vintage port – and which therefore is ready for drinking sooner, in fact as soon as it is bottled. It may bear a vintage date and the date when it was bottled. This also is a fine wine, made so that it can be easily drunk without having to be decanted, for the handling and serving of vintage port are not always everyday processes.

Crusted Port

A blend of quality ports kept in cask for, possibly, 5 or 6 years before bottling and which therefore may throw a crust. This too is a fine type of port.

Service

Apart from vintage port, which should be decanted at least an hour before serving, ruby and tawny and the others are served at the temperature of the room in which they will be drunk. White port is served chilled. Glasses should be of moderate to generous size: those used in many catering establishments are far too small for the port lover to be able to swing the wine around in the glass and enjoy its beautiful bouquet. The glorious colour of fine tawny or vintage port should be appreciated by serving such wines in clear glass or crystal, though port decanters, for which Britain is famous, are usually elaborately cut to show off the wine inside the facets of the receptacle.

Port is traditionally the wine in which the loyal toast to the sovereign is drunk at the end of special meals. But, although port is very much the 'Englishman's wine', it must be admitted that the French have drunk far more than the British in recent years, preferring it as an apéritif. They seldom drink it with dessert and indeed seldom drink vintage port. One other curious thing about a fascinating wine is that the great vintages in port in the past seldom coincide with the notable vintage years for table wines. Some of the greatest port years are those of 'off' or even non-existent years for other wines (but improved scientific vinification may change this in the future). Port, according to law, can only be sold as such if it is shipped over the 'bar' or past the spit of land outside Oporto, where the ships pass from the port.

Wines made in similar style are produced in other countries, and can achieve quality, even though they are not in any way the same thing. Some even bear vintage dates, and this can be of interest even to the most dedicated port lover. Although the wines of the Douro are now mostly produced from grafted vines as protection against the *Phylloxera*, there are some regions in the winelands of the world, such as the Hunter River in Australia, where the vines are still ungrafted and a type of port is made. Wines of port style are also made in South Africa, often making use of some of the port grapes. These can be extremely good, as are those of California.

Wines which are still, in very small quantities, made from ungrafted vines in the Douro region will have the description *nacional* on their labels. Wines, also in small quantities, which come from a single property, or *quinta*, will have this denoted on the label also. One of the most famous of these is Quinta do Noval, where a proportion of the vineyard remains planted with the old, ungrafted *nacional* stock. Other well-known *quintas* are Roeda, Vargellas, Bôa Vista, and Bomfin, to name but a few.

Port is traditionally the wine to lay down at the birth of a child (or the conception if this is a better vintage) for drinking at the twenty-first birthday. It is safe to assume that a vintage wine will be very good, even if not yet at its peak after this time; it will also be a sound investment.

SHIPS' BAPTISMS

The launch of a ship – the vessel is always referred to as 'she' – is of major importance and attended by many ceremonies. Thanks to the National Maritime Museum at Greenwich and the officer in charge of the museum now established at Portsmouth in Nelson's ship HMS *Victory* some of these traditions and observances can be traced.

For a warship, any wine poured as a celebration should always be red. The Vikings sent their warships down the slip across the bodies of their captives; a warship, tradition dictated, must smell blood at the earliest opportunity. In Tahiti, Fiji and Tonga the practice was kept up even in the nineteenth century and in 1794 the then Bey of Tunis launched cruisers with a slave tied to the prow of each. Some days were regarded as favourable to the new ship, notably Wednesday, Friday supposedly being unlucky.

In the Mediterranean a cup of wine would be poured into the sea, to placate Poseidon. The cup, of precious metal, was thrown after this offering. This depended, of course, on the wealth of the ship's owner; the custom seems to have continued until the seventeenth century. In some instances a ship would have a godfather and a godmother and, along the French coast, a new fishing boat will still often have five holes hammered into the mast, crosswise, with the holes made plugged with *pain bénit* and silver and gold coins set 'heads up' hidden in the mast step, before the mast is raised, to bring good fortune.

Throughout history, the launching of a vessel into that unknown and unpredictable element, the sea, is associated with practices that supposedly bring good fortune – such as ensuring the sun shines as the vessel enters the water. In Tudor times, states Julian Street (in *Table Topics*, 1959) there would be a spill of wine on to the deck of a new ship, and the king's health would be drunk from a golden goblet which was then thrown into the sea. There was trouble about this because one of those who had built one vessel tried to get the goblet back by means of a net and those who had hoped to go diving for it were furious. The propitiation of the sea is still continued in Cyprus, where, at Easter – in the Greek calendar – a ceremony takes place at various ports in which a cross is thrown into the sea and enthusiasts dive for it, although it is not stated that they are able to keep it if they recover it.

The tradition of a woman launching a ship obviously derives from the times when, maybe, a maiden was supposed to be associated or sacrificed with the new vessel. But the danger associated with the rush of the ship down the slip was obvious and in France in the nineteenth century convicts were deputed to chop out the last staves that held a ship from the water and any who were not killed by the vessel slipping into the sea were allowed to go free.

It is stated – by Julian Street – that the first time wine was used to 'baptise' a ship was in 1610 at Woolwich for the HMS *Princess Royal*. But the association with women launchers seems to date from 1828 for USS *Concord* by 'a young lady of Portsmouth'. But when did Champagne come into the picture? Street says that 'the steam sloop *Lackawanna* was christened with Champagne at Brooklyn Navy Yard in 1862'. Of course, this 'Champagne' might not have been 'the real thing' but the difference is important.

There are endless tales about what happened when the Champagne bottle wasn't secured to the launching pad – in early days it had just been flung at the ship. But once when the bottle hadn't been secured it hit a spectator on the head so hard that he claimed and received damages, according to *Ridley's Wine Spectator*.

Champagne bottles did present problems. Once a vessel began to slide away from the launching platform before the lady launching it had hurled the bottle; she flung it as hard as she could, but it bounced off the moving ship, was caught by the dockyard manager, who flung it back – and missed! So the VIPs had to leap into a launch and pursue the ship, and succeeded in doing so. (But ever since, bottles of Champagne are usually weighted so that they break at the first impact on the new ship.)

Once, when the then Japanese Minister of Marine was launching a ship the bottle swung short of the vessel and hung by its ribbon. Before the vessel reached the water, a sampan rushed up alongside, cut the ribbon and went off with the bottle!

There are numerous accounts of how ships were launched in North America. In early times there might be a mix of wine and water from the river on which the ship was named. The first time the *Constitution* was supposed to be launched at Boston, water was brought into use to baptise the ship, but the attempt failed on two counts, and it was only when a bottle of Madeira was put to use that the launching was successful. Sometimes it seems that rum was used and, in 1863, the USS *Shamrock* was launched with Irish whiskey.

There have also been instances when 'temperance beverages' have been used to launch ships, but this seems to have been a forerunner of misfortune. In 1853, the largest vessel in the world at that time was supposed to be launched with Cochituate water, brought to Boston by the builder of the clipper, Donald McKay, who had hoped to gain the support of the temperance movement by publicising this. However, the night before the launching some of the apprentices in the shipyard had got hold of the Champagne intended for the launch and drank it – McKay didn't replace it. *The Great Republic* caught fire soon after loading and also caused fires on two clippers nearby – a moral tale, said all concerned, because McKay should not have been so mean as to have failed to replace the Champagne.

It is fair to say that the launch of any vessel is still associated with a certain solemnity; the voice of Queen Mary, consort of George V, was heard for the only time on microphone when she named the great Cunarder.

NAPOLEON'S DRINKS AT WATERLOO

The great Napoleon Bonaparte was a genius at many things – but was not noted as a connoisseur of food and wine. Brought up in Corsica – where even today many wines tend to be of the 'enjoyable on holiday' type – he may have been lucky to get enough to eat while at military academy and in the French army. True, he is credited with the

Napoleon Bonaparte (1769–1821). If you were invited to dinner with Napoleon, you made sure you had a meal before you went! (*Private Collection/Bridgeman Art Library*)

saying that 'An army marches on its stomach', but this is also said to have been of the opinion of Frederick the Great of Prussia. Neither of them achieved renown as givers of great dinners. Indeed, the great chef Câreme thought Napoleon was a coarse eater and said that he rushed through meals at such a pace – often grabbing at any of the dishes on the table as he felt inclined – that some of those invited to have dinner with him often prudently dined before they came.

However, Napoleon did realise that good food and wine were important in negotiations, and that strange man Charles Maurice de Talleyrand Périgord (1754–1838), who slithered from one allegiance to another, saw that much may be achieved around a good table. Talleyrand came, originally as a fairly humble attendant at the Congress of Vienna in 1815, but at the end he had achieved diplomatic triumph after triumph. The diary of Frances, Lady Shelley, who surveyed all the great personalities of the early nineteenth century, noted that, when Talleyrand entertained in Paris 'the antiquities of every bottle of wine supplied the most eloquent annotations'. Napoleon might have been bored, Talleyrand's guests were not.

Napoleon, though, liked red Burgundy. The full, slightly plumped out wine, thanks to the work of Chaptal, was able to make an obvious appeal. When he went over to the Egyptian campaign, Napoleon's secretary noted that the wines taken by the top brass didn't suffer from being shipped across the Mediterranean and 'several boxes of this Burgundy twice crossed the desert on camelback and some which we brought with us on our return to Fréjus', where they had set sail, 'was as good as when we started.'

Desmond Flower, in the magazine *Wine & Food*, notes that 'there were no wine cellars in the Tuileries or any of the palaces'. (One assumes that, during the French Revolution, the cellars, if they did hold stocks, were sacked and the wine drunk up by the mob.) Since then, it would appear that wine was supplied on a 'sale or return' basis, and it is curious that 'like all the wines and liqueurs used in the palaces it was sent in porcelain bottles made at Sèvres with the Imperial cipher'. A lot of showing-off, not much knowledge.

Napoleon, the same authority mentions, liked drinks chilled 'and usually diluted with water'. And, one may at least guess, he would have found red Burgundy acceptable if offered it on the campaign when he invaded Russia. In 1812 General de Coulaincourt, with the Army, wrote that although the Cossacks had plundered some of the supplies that had been sent in advance, Napoleon did get his Burgundy and 'Clos Vougeot and Chambertin were the common drink'. Coulaincourt was invited to dine by the French minister when the Army paused at Warsaw, but the invitation was declined with a 'Send a bottle of Burgundy there' to the rather poor hotel where Napoleon was obliged to stay. (Napoleon's preference for red Burgundy is said to be because he thought it encouraged the conception of male children.)

However, after Waterloo, Napoleon's carriage was captured and it was found and reported that he had drunk most of a bottle of Malaga and the same amount of rum. He must have felt the need for something sweet and warming. But the appalling affliction from which he suffered and which prevented him from being on horseback, ahead of his men, throughout that terrible day, was haemorrhoids. Although William of Orange, later William III, had the same problem, he did not have to endure the very long sessions involving the tremendous manoeuvrings of the Army that confronted Napoleon. (No such affliction concerned the Duke of Wellington.)

On St Helena, Napoleon shared the dislike of the Governor, Sir Hudson Lowe, that one of Wellington's staff had earlier recorded. Yet, when Napoleon died, in 1821, his household had consignments of 'wines, clarets, graves, Champagnes and madeira'. Unfortunately none of those who devotedly accompanied Napoleon were even vaguely interested in wine or cooking. Yet this was the time when the Cape vineyards were beginning to produce wines, such as Groot Constantia, famous throughout the world. None of Napoleon's entourage seems to have been interested in making the best of their situation – nor of interesting themselves in food and wine, Alas!

... AND THE ABSTEMIOUS WELLINGTON

When Brevet Colonel Arthur Wellesley of the 33rd Regiment returned from India, he spent several months at the Cape. The young officer kept mainly to his rooms, engaged in study – he assigned regular hours to this daily – but he did often visit Cape Town to dine with a Mr Walker. This gentleman was very hospitable and on many occasions his guests had to be provided with beds so as to sleep off the effects of the hospitality. Arthur Wellesley, however, is recorded as never having been noted to 'take over-much wine and always rode home by himself'! He is said to have liked 'both the Pontac and Madeira from Mr Cloete's farm very much'.

When Wellesley sailed back to England in 1805 he went ashore at St Helena and found it beautiful and with a 'delightful climate', although he found the then Governor extremely eccentric. Subsequently, in Portugal he kept a pack of hounds and delighted in 'a

The Duke of Wellington (1769–1852), circle of Sir Thomas Lawrence. Though personally very abstemious, fine wines were always served at his table. (*Bonhams, London/Bridgeman Art Library*)

good gallop'. He was, says Christopher Hibbert, in *Wellington, a personal history* (1998), 'at his desk writing until nine o'clock when he had breakfast, a spare, plain meal as all his meals usually were . . . and was little concerned if he passed twenty-fours hours without eating anything at all other than the crust and boiled egg he sometimes stuffed into his pocket when riding out of a morning.' One Spanish gentleman was horrified when asking about the time they were to set off and what they would have for dinner, he received the reply 'At daylight. Cold meat.' The great Duke de Cambacérès, a famous gourmet, was appalled to be informed by the Duke of Wellington that 'I don't care much what I eat'.

Later, in retirement, he was reported as eating fast but not much, 'mixing meat, rice and vegetables into a mess on his plate', according to Lord Ellesmere. But the wines served at his table were invariably first-rate and the Duke was firm that 'I made it a point to pay my own bills.' He drank little wine but much iced water, two decanters of which were put beside him and which were usually emptied by the time he went to bed.

The last words he spoke were, 'Yes, if you please' when asked if he would like a cup of tea. But he didn't drink it.

Fine Wines for a Man-of-War

 Bills and accounts can often be revealing: the pinnace that went after the Royal Navy when it had sailed for what was to be the Battle of Trafalgar in 1805 took wines but not more than a few bottles of Champagne – why? But of course, in those days the corks of the superb wine were tied down with cord, not wire, as today, and the motion of the vessel might have accentuated the pressure behind the corks. Even until recently those visiting Champagne cellars might risk the danger of some bottles exploding, and at least one cellar provided fencing masks for its distinguished guests.

The use of fine wines aboard a man-of-war was a medicinal as well as a social commodity. Nelson's accounts of his sickness at sea are well known and, when a warship went into action, the decks would be painted red, so that the surgeons could do their horrid work without alarming the crew too much.

BORDEAUX 'TONNAGE' AND THE ARMING OF THE NAVY

During the period when the English owned the south-west of France, the ships engaged in taking wine to various markets, including the northern capitals but, pre-eminently, to England, would race to get first to the overseas buyers anxious to obtain the first samples. In London the 'bouteiller' or butler of the reigning monarch had first choice when the vessels arrived in the port of London.

The gigantic casks that were rolled into the ships' holds were 'tonnes' or, latterly, tuns, so that it became the standard measurement of a sea-going ship to use this statement of capacity – as it is today. The original 'tonne' held 252 gallons and the use of this term survives – a reminder of the way in which the wine trade established a usage of what a ship might hold.

Another wisp of tradition that was established during this time was when the wine fleet risked being attacked *en route* when returning from Bordeaux by the pirates that lurked around the Brittany coast. So vessels whisking down to Bordeaux and hurrying back with their precious casks began to carry a few men-at-arms on board to deal with marauders. Maybe this was when the ships of the English king began to be armed – and the tradition of the Royal Navy was established. Anyway, it's pleasing to think that it may have been the protection of cargoes of wine that incited ships officially to bear arms.

FOUR

ENEMIES OF WINE

AGE: FRIEND OR FOE?

Wines are rather like people: some are at their best and most enjoyable when young, others can achieve great interest with age. But it's important to know the purpose for which they have been made. For example, in former times – say pre-1939 – many of the 'classic' red wines of Bordeaux and Burgundy might either be shipped in bulk – that is to say in cask – after undergoing fermentation or, if they were very special, they could be bottled at the property where they were made; yet the procedure of bottling might take two to three months in the days before mechanisation was installed.

In the past, of course, before wine went into bottles, it was the new or young wine that was sought after; the days when the wine fleets raced each other to get to the northern ports so as to unload for the innkeepers and the nobility were obvious. Later, when certain wines, such as those of Bordeaux, were able to develop wonderfully in the bottle, even Burgundies and red wines of other regions were able to display shades of difference that delighted those able to afford them.

An old wine of a certain area and of a certain vintage can provide a revelation of enjoyment to some drinkers. But these are the rarities today. Sometimes wine is dredged from shipwrecked vessels or dug up

An historic vintage bottle of Château Lafite, 1803, surrounded by some of the leaves of the vines from which it is made. (© *Christie's Images Ltd, 2002*)

from ancient buildings, from before London's Great Fire. Laboratories have often established that, yes, the liquid sealed within such containers could be defined as 'wine'. But as no one knows the condition of the beverage when it went into bottle – or amphora – or any other container, one cannot be definite.

It has sometimes been possible to drink a wine cherished for much longer in its cask than would occur today, when greater knowledge of the way wine matures is part of the education of those who work in the wine world. For age, in itself, it is not necessarily an advantage; a wine that may have been delicious when within two to three years of its vintage may sag into dreariness as it ages. Also, in former times, such as the 'historic' wines written about in the memoirs of many older wine scribes, would have remained in the initial stages of their lives for much longer – certain reds, for example, might have remained in cask for three or four years, rather than the two which many experience today. With white wines their potential for improving with age may not be as great as with the classic reds, so it is important to check with the source of supply – if possible an informed wine merchant who knows the stock he or she sells – and the preferences of the customer.

Wine is to be enjoyed. Many people snobbishly boast about trying old wines, or even how they have tried very young ones. It's up to them! Certain wines can remain capable of providing enjoyment for many years, others fade and become flabby within a short while. This is the sort of thing that can only be subject to experience. One much respected friend once pronounced: 'I prefer to sample the early bottles from the bottling line – but I'd rather drink a sample from the tank waiting to fill them!' There is no right and wrong about this – any more than there is about people. But it is worth trying what ageing can do to wines, even cheap wines: do they become flabby, dull and lacking in smell? Drink them up! But with certain wines, it is worth seeing what careful handling, possibly decanting or a little aeration may do to them: rather like releasing the genie from the bottle, a wonderful surprise may await the drinker who has been lucky and has possibly taken advice from someone informed.

So – remember when reading older wine writers, that some of the wines they found wonderful may have waited for years before they were bottled or, then, remained in a re-corked bottle after even more than a century. That can be a great experience. It doesn't mean it will or can happen every day! With medium range and cheap wines, don't expect them to get past their peak of enjoyment. With anything rather special – take advice and follow it. But don't necessarily wait too long!

The Calendar

Anyone researching old wines should be aware of the way in which the calendar varied in different regions.

As wine regions dated their produce – in the days when wine was often valued because it was young rather than old – it was according to calendars in use locally.

The Julian calendar was established by Julius Caesar and was kept, with various adjustments, in Roman Catholic Europe until 1582, when Pope Gregory XIII corrected it. The British didn't follow this calendar until 1752 and then there was fierce opposition from those who supposed themselves to be deprived of some days and appeals to 'Give us back our eleven days!' caused much dissension. So, always check which calendar was in use at the time the wine was produced.

'CORKED' AND 'CORKY'

Many bottles are taken back to suppliers as 'corked'; often, unfortunately, the drinker may simply not like the wine or, having opened the bottle, immediately reacted to its contents, when the 'bottle stink' or stale air retained in the top of the bottle just under the cork can affect the initial impression of the smell and taste. It must be stressed that not only can opinions vary enormously, even among authorities, but only an interval will enable true 'corkiness' to develop – and then it is definite and so unpleasant that people will not wish to drink the wine. (Curiously, if, as a guest, one has to pass as 'all right' a wine that really is not what it should be, one never feels quite tranquil inside afterwards: corkiness won't hurt the drinker, it just won't make him or her feel comfortable.)

To distinguish true faults in a wine needs some knowledge and study: so often a wine that is personally not to the taste of the drinker may be rejected, but on several occasions when I was trying to be a wine waiter, the rejected bottles – which I naturally replaced with something else – were those I drank for my supper, and were perfectly all right, the drinkers either having had the wrong sort of apéritifs or snacks or just not liking the wine.

WINE DEPOSITS

Several world-famous authorities on wine have written about deposits, both those that are formed in the cask or the vat and those that occur once the wine is bottled. It is a specialised subject and one that need not affect the lover of wine as a rule. In the past, wines were often bottled without being filtered and some very fine wines today are allowed time to 'fall bright' prior to being bottled. But as, obviously, no drinker wants a glass of wine to be full of sludge, more care is taken today to ensure that, certainly with many wines, the result after bottling is 'star bright'.

In the past – certainly prior to 1914 – many table wines might stay in their casks or vats for far longer than they do today: claret, for example, is generally bottled at or within two years of its vintage at the great Bordeaux estates. But, occasionally, somebody may be given a very old wine as a treat, and this sometimes may have remained in its cask for three or even four years. This may not, it must be stressed, make the wine 'better' – it will inevitably make it different.

Even today many people become suspicious when they see, for example, a few shiny crystals on the cork of a wine – nothing wrong with that; indeed, the wine is likely to be of quality. The same applies to the slightly shiny crystals that may lurk in the bottom of the bottle: they are tartrates and can be eaten, if anyone doubts, without the slightest danger; they are there because the wine hasn't had the guts knocked out of it by excessive filtration.

Of course, no wine should present a cloudy, dusty, dull appearance. Yet most, if properly handled, need not inflict this on the drinker. With old wines – when the deposit may be seen in the bottle – standing the bottle up or sensitive decanting can obviate such a problem. What many people do not realise is that, if they buy fine wine from a wine merchant, they should be willing and able to decant the wine before any important function, as this is advisable. (Deposit that cannot be eked into a cautiously held glass after decanting is completed can go into the vinegar jar, or even be drunk up.)

PROHIBITION

This is the term for the time when parts of the United States 'went dry'. Certain states had in fact set up tough legislation about the use and sale of alcoholic beverages earlier, but it was in 1920, shortly after the end of World War I, that some would-be do-gooders got the idea that soldiers returning from the war must be protected against the excesses of alcohol. Of course, exactly the opposite occurred and the rise of gangsterdom supplying 'bootleg' liquor of all kinds caused terrible drinks to be made – mixed up in bathtubs – and there were intimidating ladies going around breaking up bottles and pouring any-thing alcoholic into the drains. It has been pertinently said that, because of the very dubious nature of many such drinks, the cocktail and the mixed drink came into society. At least some mixes can be pleasant.

The era lasted until 1933, but there are many areas in the world today where alcoholic drinks are pro-hibited including some Islamic countries. An authority

Emptying wine down a drain in the street during prohibition. (© *Bettmann/CORBIS*)

on Muslim culture has stressed that it is not the use but the abuse of alcohol that is deplored, but it's a cosmic twist of history that countries where the art of distillation was evolved – to make perfume – and the grape grows in abundance, should now have in place restrictions on the use of alcohol.

MILDEW

This is one of the great enemies to vines and it is often known as *Oïdium tuckerii*, because, in 1845, it was the gardener to a Mr Tucker, at Margate, who discovered it in his vine house. It probably arrived in Britain from America. By 1832 virtually all the vineyards of Europe and North Africa were trying to deal with this pest, which attacks the leaves of the vine. Fortunately, it was discovered that dusting with sulphur checks the mildew and protects the vine – this is why sulphur is still much used in vineyards to this day. The great authority George Ordish noted that, in the mid-nineteenth century, many of the vines trained over porches and along trellises in country houses fell victim to this mildew and, dying off as they did, gave credence to the belief that vines could not flourish in many parts of England.

It is important not to confuse powdery mildew with *phylloxera*; the latter attacks the roots of the vine. Mildew can be kept under control by spraying, although during World War II the difficulty in obtaining sulphur was a serious matter to owners of vineyards.

PHYLLOXERA AND THE GREAT WINE PLAGUE

Anyone visiting vineyards will probably hear of the great wine plague, *Phylloxera vastatrix*, that attacked the roots of vines in the middle of the nineteenth century. It was first noted in Hammersmith in 1863 and it spread rapidly, so much so that

European vineyards would have been completely destroyed had researches not established that the aphis does not attack vines grafted on to American rootstock. The life cycle of the aphis is unusual, but has been thoroughly chronicled by my late dear friend, George Ordish, in *The Great Wine Blight* (1972).

The only way to combat the aphis is by flooding the vineyard; the aphis does not like sandy soils, so that the vineyards planted on sand continue on their own rootstock. There are, though, vineyards in the New World where the *Phylloxera* has never struck, so that ungrafted vines are planted, but the possible threat is always present and some vineyards may be grafted anyway.

There is also a slight but definite difference that can be noticed in wines made from grafted or ungrafted vinestocks. Grapes from ungrafted vines produce a juice and, therefore, a wine that is fuller, softer and with more shades of bouquet and taste. Indeed, there are a few vineyards where, even with the *Phylloxera* rampant, owners have opted for keeping these vines in production, even though, to the outsider, they will look somewhat shabby; however, with the possible cost of replanting – something that might have been ruinous to owners in the past – this is one view of dealing with the plague. For, once in the soil, *Phylloxera* cannot be eradicated, unless by flooding the vineyard – hardly practical or economic!

CASKS

It should be understood that, with anything made by the hands of craftsmen, such as coopers, slight variations in contenance must occur. With a 'château barrel' which may be used for shipping, even in these days, the contenance may be slightly different from one cask to another. A 'château barrel' will, obviously, be slightly different from a barrel used for transporting wine, and the exact size may vary slightly.

Casks in the Adega of the Quinta da Bôa Vista, Alto Douro.

Many visitors to great wine estates will indeed see rows of casks trimly sited on the scantling, as they expected, when the wine is to be shipped it may well be put into something less picturesque – such as a tank. There is nothing suspicious in this. Only a very few fine wines able to mature interestingly by being kept in wood – casks – can be given the time to mature in this way and they will, nowadays, usually remain in the cellars where they originally went into the casks.

It should be borne in mind, however, that ageing in wood, for certain wines, is not always likely to make them more enjoyable to drinkers of today, who want the wines to be fresh and appealing.

SIPHONS, VELENCHE AND VENENCIA

In the past, wine went into casks of various kinds – the size might be peculiar to different countries and regions. But, once in, how was the wine to be removed? A very few casks might be fitted with a spigot and a tap, but this was not an ideal way of sampling before the wine might be ready to try or actually enjoy. By the time the casks were resting on the scantling – the wooden supports – in a cellar, they would be 'bung up', because the process of fermentation would be completed or nearly so and the bung hole, with the stopper of the bung itself, would be at the highest point of the cask. It would not be easy to secure supplies unless the container was almost full. Even if someone just got wet trying to get some of the liquid out of the container, they would be sticky and, should the wine be undergoing a stage of fermentation, merely to breathe in any gases given off on the surface could be dangerous.

In case this should sound dramatic, it ought to be known that in wine regions where the containers for holding wine are large there is a strict rule that no one goes into a vat or big cask, even when this is virtually empty, without having a rope around him – or her – so that, if overcome by the fumes, those outside can pull up the body before it becomes a corpse – which has been known to occur. Indeed, a well-regulated winery will make a rule that no one goes alone into a vat or tank – there must always be two or more.

Even a small quantity of liquid in the bottom of a cask will keep the staves tight, so that, without a tap being fitted, wine cannot be obtained except from the surface of the container. To dip a small vessel through the bunghole was the obvious answer. Known by the French word 'velenche', or as a 'pipette', 'sonde' or, even 'thief', the device consists of a glass or metal cylinder, with a spout at one end and open at the other, plus a hooked loop whereby the device is prevented from falling into the cask if it is left alone. The procedure is that the velenche is plunged into the wine via the bunghole, then the cylinder is allowed to fill with wine, after which the open end is stopped by applying the thumb to the opening. The velenche, holding the wine, may then be drawn out of the cask and, when held over a glass or similar receptacle, slight release of the seal over the top will cause wine to flow into the designated container. The thumb can reseal the velenche until more wine is to be released.

The procedure seems difficult but in fact is quite easy. In cellars where casks of sizes larger than the usual hogshead are in use, of course a velenche with a long stem has to be employed. Because of the depth of the wine in the casks this is sometimes the length of an arm or even longer. Curiously, the way in which the wine can be lifted from a larger container was also known in Britain by those who made 'toddy lifters', which are small hollow-stemmed glass vessels that could be plunged into a mixed drink of toddy or punch, stoppered with the thumb while being lifted and then the liquid directed wherever it was required.

Even when there was no surface formation on the top of the wine – as with 'flor' in sherry – disturbance of the surface of a wine undergoing development is not wise. So as little disturbance as possible was required should wine, at any stage of its development, have to be drawn from where it is lying.

The venenciador filling several glasses from the venencia, which has been dipped into the butt of sherry. (*Mick Rock/Cephas*)

With sherry, a different sort of device is necessary because, with a wine that has grown a mass of flor on its surface in cask, this should not be disturbed. So the *capataz* or head of a sherry *bodega* uses a venencia. This is a narrow metal cup on a flexible whalebone handle. The venencia pierces the surface of the wine without disturbing the flor and then samples can be poured as required. The *capataz* is often capable of amazing dexterity with the venencia, whirling it round his head before pouring, never spilling a drop. It is not unknown for a *capataz* accustomed to giving a little show for visitors to hold as many as thirteen *copitas* of sherry in one hand, while whirling the venencia around with the other and directing the wine into each of the glasses, without a drop being spilled.

BOTTLES: SHAPES AND SIZES

The word 'bottle' is old but, as it begins to be used in Middle English, it derives from the French '*bouteiller*'. The container implied is one with a narrow neck and, in former times, the containers for liquid were often leather, other substances being fragile. This is why the 'leather bottle' features in some folk songs. As glass became known as a useful receptacle for wine, a variety of bottles came into use. Of course, it was not until the mid-nineteenth century that wine was routinely put into bottles for subsequent maturation and, it was hoped, for improvement. Prior to that, the bottle was more like a carafe, into which wine could be drawn from the cask in the cellar and then brought to the table. But with the realization of the use of cork as a seal, bottle makers increased in number. It was obvious that they would encourage local business, and there were a number in Bordeaux to facilitate the post-Napoleonic trade in French wines.

Bottles were not standardised until quite recent times, and convenience dictated the shape of most of them. Show-off customers of an importer would often have their own device moulded into the glass of the bottle and simply send their required number to the merchant or importer when it was necessary to order fresh supplies. Samuel Pepys did this. The size of bottles could vary, so that it is uncertain as to whether a Regency buck boasting of his capacity as a 'three bottle

English wine bottles of the seventeenth and eighteenth centuries used for drawing wine from the cellar. (*Royal Albert Memorial Museum, Exeter/ Bridgeman Art Library*)

man' could drink the contents of three bottles such as we use today. (And it is pertinent to comment that many of the older wine glasses held only smallish measures of wine.)

The makers of bottles, too, might not always keep to an exact measure and, understandably, they produced bottles likely to be of use in the regions nearby where wines were made. The shape and the contours of the bottle were what the local wines required: white wines, throwing little or no deposit, went into bottles with flat bases, those that usually threw a heavy deposit had a punt or indentation at the base in which this deposit might be collected, and with wines throwing a firm deposit, there would usually be a shoulder to hold back this deposit when the wine was poured. Similarly, bottles for wine intended to be kept for some time might be of darker-toned glass, so as to protect the wine from light.

These days inexpensive wines may be bottled by the firm which ships them, so that it is up to the bottler to decide on the shape that may appeal to the public. In very general terms, the use of the sloping-shouldered Burgundy-style bottle, where any deposit tends to be light and fairly unobtrusive will be used for many wines, whereas the square-shouldered Bordeaux-style bottle, where any harder deposit can be seen around the base of the bottle, will be utilised for wines that may throw a deposit on occasion, when it is thought that the appeal of this type of bottle will be effective.

Today, most bottles are standardised, although some special wines such as Château Chalon (63 cl.), may be exempted even from the EC regulations. Although bottles are subject to legislation, it is a fair generalisation to say that, nowadays, most will contain about 73/75 centilitres. Of course, much depends as to whether some of the wine in the bottle has evaporated. Champagne bottles hold 60/81 centilitres. With large bottles, the following are a guide: in Champagne, a magnum holds the equivalent of two bottles; a jeroboam, 4 bottles; a rehoboam, 6 bottles; a methuselah, 8 bottles; a salmanazar, 12 bottles; a balthazar, 16 bottles; a nebuchadnezzar, 20 bottles. No one knows how the huge bottles acquired their names. A Bordeaux jeroboam used to hold 5 bottles until 1978, but it now holds 5 litres (6.67 bottles). An impériale holds 8 bottles.

Anyone wishing to check on the current capacity of wine bottles should consult the Wine Standards Board of the Vintners' Company, Five Kings House, 1 Queen Street Place, London EC4R 1QS.

DECANTERS AND DECANTING

The first form of a decanter in Britain was probably a jug or flask, used to bring the wine required from either the store or cellar. It didn't always have a stopper, and might also do duty as a carafe for water. Decanters with ample bowls became decorated and they also became identifiable by the 'bottle ticket' that was hung on a chain around the decanter neck and spelled out what was in the decanter. The great achievements of British glass-makers showed in decanters elegant and beautiful in shape and proportion; they were sometimes cut decoratively, but also engraved with many devices and patterns.

Although there seems to be no convention about certain decanters having square shoulders, it does seem that wines that did not throw a deposit and might be situated on the sideboard, for occasional refreshment, such as Madeira, sherry and even ordinary ports, did often have decanters with dumpier proportions rather than swan-necked wine decanters. In the nineteenth century bottles intended for wine were often set into a tantalus, or frame, which could be locked so that no one could pilfer the wines. The name derives from Tantalus, son of Zeus and a nymph, who revealed the secrets of the gods to mortals. As a punishment he was hanged up

Heavily cut and engraved decanter and glass, for which British glassworks became famous. This is from a nineteenth-century service by Baccarat. (*Museum of London/Bridgeman Art Library*)

to the chin in a river of Hades, with beautiful fruits just above him that receded when he tried to pick them.

In the twentieth century decanters holding whisky, gin and possibly sherry tended to be chunkier in form – they did not have to be passed with any attempt at grace when on the table and therefore it was only necessary to have a decanter of some solidity, that could be easily grasped for pouring.

A 'ship' decanter is one that is almost triangular in the bowl, so as to give it moderate steadiness aboard ship. Certain port decanters had rounded bowls, so that they could not be set down until they had gone round the table and reached the host, who would have a frame in which to hold such a vessel known as a hogget.

Decanting is the simple procedure of pouring wine off from any accumulated deposit in the bottom of the bottle. It also serves to aerate the wine, which can be

Silver wine funnels for use in decanting. Note the way the funnels are curved to avoid the wine falling straight down into the decanter, where it might splash and cause too much aeration. The wine should run quietly down the side of the decanter. (*S.J. Shrobsole Ltd/ Bridgeman Art Library*)

advantageous with certain wines which need, as it were, 'waking up' to release their smell as well as their flavour. Until recently decanting funnels were used but they are seldom seen these days. The point of the spout is angled to one side, so that the wine cannot be poured straight into the decanter. It goes without saying that any such device must be kept scrupulously clean. Years ago, some would decant through clean muslin or linen, putting this in the frame of a fine-meshed filter.

CRACKING A BOTTLE

This expression, today, signifies opening a bottle of wine. But it was rather more dramatic in the past, when the main part of the neck of the bottle was actually removed by making a crack around it.

The necessity for doing this probably occurred most often with vintage port; the neck of a bottle of vintage port is very slightly bulbous, giving the cork extra space in which to expand. But after some years the cork might be fragile and liable to crumble so that, in establishments where much port was drunk, bottle tongs would often be employed. The tongs are metal, with two arms arranged so as to grip around the neck of the bottle, but with separate handles, so that they could be gripped when the tongs were heated. The tongs, made hot in the fire, grip the neck of the bottle and then it is cracked cleanly off. But, as might be expected, there is a way of doing this: the bottle stands upright and then, at the point where the crack is to be made, a band of fine cloth, such as linen, soaked in cold water, is wound firmly around the bottle-neck. Then the heated tongs are applied to this and, like magic, the glass will crack and the section of the bottle's neck, plus the cork, can be lifted off safely. The wine can then be decanted from the remains of the bottle and although it is unlikely that there will be any splinters of glass around the crack, care should obviously be taken.

These days, with improved corkscrews and many wines not throwing such heavy deposits as they did in the past, it is unusual to need to take the neck off a bottle of vintage port or old claret – but this is how our ancestors performed the task.

CORKS AND STOPPERS

The cork oak, *quercus suber*, has been growing in certain parts of Europe for many years. It is not recorded whether the wine makers of ancient times used it, but before there were radical changes in the European climate it may even have been known in England. Today, the main source for cork is Catalonia, and it is thought that the monks of the Benedictine monastery of Hautvillers, in the heart of the Champagne region, may have used it to stopper their wine flasks as they trekked between the various monasteries of their order. Prior to this period, flasks and such bottles as did exist were probably just stoppered with a scrap of oily cloth, rammed into the neck of the container. In more ancient times amphorae and similar flasks would be sealed with pitch.

After the bark of the cork oak is stripped from a mature tree, the tree must have a period of a further eight to nine years before more bark can be taken without harming the tree. The cork that has been stripped is cut into sections, boiled and then, if top quality corks are required, it is left to mature out of doors. Corks are cut by hand for the finest wines, but all corks must be trimmed and cleaned, so that the markings of the grain are removed. Before being used for wine, quality corks will be sterilised.

With Champagne and sparkling wines it is important that the 'cork', which is often composed of many layers, should have the finer type of cork as the layer that is actually in contact with the wine. Although I have been assured that, for the very finest wines, certain establishments do not use the type of cork that is composed of layers stuck together, with a top 'mushroom' made from morsels of cork bound together, but one solid piece of cork, I have not seen this myself. It may still be so. But most sparkling wines will be stoppered with corks composed of several layers.

There are various sizes of corks, according to the use to which they will be put. Wine intended for long-term maturation will usually be about 2 in. long and will mostly be hand-cut. But this rather depends on the quality of the wine destined for the bottle and a 'full long' cork these days will only be used for the finest wines. A 'short long' cork of 1¾ in. may be used for other good but not especially fine wines. Fine red

Bordeaux and Burgundy may be sealed with the Bordeaux cork, which is about ⅞ in.

These days many different types of stopper are utilised to seal bottles of wine, including the 'stopper cork' which has a metal or plastic top above the actual cork. Sparkling wines are stoppered with a cork that is levered into the bottle rim to maintain the seal. Many world-famous wine estates have corks branded with the name of the property. A Champagne cork is usually branded on its base, although sometimes there is also a brand on the side of the cork.

The use of plastic for sealing many inexpensive wines today should not be despised – although it is difficult to extract the corkscrew itself from some of these.

CORKSCREWS

 Sometimes this appliance is referred to as a 'bottlescrew', but it was an inevitable tool for extracting corks once corks were driven home. It is possible that the earliest reference to what we should recognise as a corkscrew occurred in 1681 as 'a steel worm used for the drawing of Corks out of Bottles'. The cult of the corkscrew varied according to where it was to be used and there is an infinite variety of styles, some with adjuncts such as a brush, used for brushing away the wax that might have been used to seal the bottle, or various frames or holders whereby the neck of the bottle is held firm while the corkscrew is inserted. There are many types of 'extractors' to facilitate the removal of the cork, and there are literally hundreds of the devices, some of them fetching high prices in the salerooms, and societies concerned with the accumulation of cork extractors of many kinds have been formed.

Many corkscrews sold today are virtually gimlets, only useful for piercing a hole in an object; if used on a

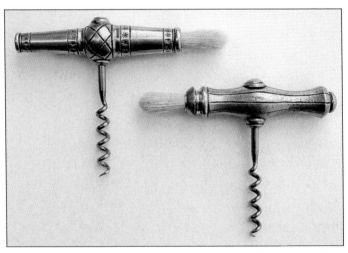

Corkscrews, each with a rounded spiral that does not end in a point, which would merely pierce the cork, not grip it. The brush serves to remove any wax with which the bottle may have been sealed and which should be knocked away before the corkscrew is inserted. (*Birchgrove Products Ltd, Guildford*)

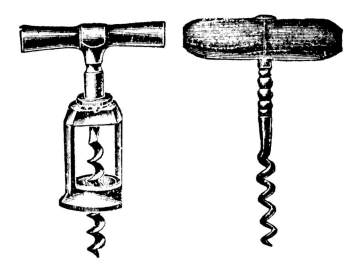

Old corkscrews, one able to fit over the top of a bottle.

cork, they may go through it but will not grip and hold it so that it may then be pulled away from the bottle. A good corkscrew should have a curled screw with rounded edges, the end of the screw being like a spiral, so that one can look up it. The screw itself should be of moderate length, but this rather depends on the sort of corks it is destined to pull – 'full long' corks need a longer 'worm' than more everyday wines. But the important thing is that, once inserted, the corkscrew should hold the cork and respond to a pull. If a cork is very old or of indifferent quality, of course, it may crumble and then the person holding the corkscrew must either attempt to dig the rest of the cork out, gently, or else to push the cork into the wine and then decant, letting the bits of cork remain in any funnel, or sieve, which should be completely clean.

Many modern corkscrews have been designed to make it possible even for those with weak or elderly hands to extract the cork from the bottle with a minimum of effort. If the wine bottle itself is handled with care, there need be no hesitation about using them.

COCONUT DRINKING CUPS

 In the early days of settlers in North America coconuts were sometimes used to serve as drinking vessels. Since very early times, states Alice Morse Earle in *Home Life in Colonial Days* (1898), coconuts had been 'mounted in metal and sometimes with a wooden handle the coconut cups or "dippers" as they are referred to were popular'. Of course, they were hard wearing!

The drinking mugs of the English settlers were often of stoneware, made in England and in Germany and the 'oldest authenticated drinking vessel in this country . . . was the property of Governor John Winthrop, who came to Boston in 1630'. This pot has a silver lid and is silver-mounted.

A seventeenth-century coconut cup and cover. (*S.J. Phillips, London/Bridgeman Art Library*)

THE PORRON

The Spanish word is pronounced with the accent on the second syllable. The porron is a drinking vessel that derives from the wineskin, although these days it may be glass, pottery or even

An elaborate and heavily decorated eighteenth-century Catalonian porron. (*Hermitage, St Petersburg/Bridgeman Art Library*)

china. It may be engraved or hung about with objects supposed to increase consumption of the wine within. Essentially, it is triangular, with a fairly broad base, tapering up to the opening at the top, through which the wine is poured. The neck is narrow but, halfway down the side of the main body of the vessel, there is a spout that projects outwards. This is so that wine or any other liquid may be poured directly to the drinker, either into the drinking vessel or, as would have happened with the wineskin, into his mouth. The need for drinkers to avoid their mouths contacting what might be a source of infection was recognised from early times. Sometimes, depending on the character of the restaurant, the wine waiter using the porron might decide to provide some entertainment and to demonstrate his skill by directing the stream of liquid from the spout of the porron into a glass via his forehead, nose, or simply direct the flow from high above his head. The changing direction of the stream of liquid is part of the entertainment and, of course, none should be misdirected so as to spill. The use of the porron – which aerates the wine of course – is common in southern Spain. In the north, more conventional vessels are used.

GLASSES: SHAPES AND SIZES

Those who see historic glasses or, sometimes, are asked to drink from them by those who prize them, may be astonished to note that the size of the bowl is usually small and, often, the rim curves outwards. Even glasses traditional in some wine regions may seem, by the critical standards of today, to be both too small, too thick and of the wrong shape.

Various types of wine glasses.

There are several reasons for this. The incurving bowl of the wine glass was something that developed only fairly recently in terms of wine – about a century or so ago! It resulted from the time when wines, now able to develop in bottle, possessed additional aromas, which the glass could capture if the rim curved inwards. With some wines, where the immediate enjoyment of their fragrance and flavour might be obvious, the capturing of the smell in the bowl of the wine was not of importance. True, today certain wines may develop fascinating additional fragrance if they are left to be swirled in a glass, but traditional glasses, such as for many white or sparkling wines, usually give pleasant fragrance immediately, not needing to wait to be swirled – or not much. So the outcurving brim, signifying the wine's fragrance being immediately available, was an asset.

Straight-sided glasses also did not usually hold very much in their bowls. The cutting of patterns on the glass was a business for the local glassworks and, of course, the glass itself had to be thick enough to take the cutting. Engraving and cutting enhanced the look of glasses. In the mid-nineteenth century, too, many wines that would have featured at important tables would have been German – colourless. The influence of the Court was not strong as regards wine, but certainly Queen Victoria and those round her drank German wines. The sorts of foods eaten would, too, be of a type partnered by this type of wine (the great roasts and pies, and even casseroles were inclined to be the fare of countryfolk or such aristocrats as dined at their own houses rather than the Court) – and be portions of something somewhat insipid. It was in the mid-nineteenth century that more diners began to understand how wine might develop and appeal to drinkers after it had been bottled and then decanted. This was when dining clubs began to extend their scope from places where men plotted or threw away fortunes at the gaming table and as a refuge from domesticity. What many of the well-to-do required was somewhere to drink: they couldn't go to the local drinking dens, so they enjoyed themselves at their clubs.

British glassware enjoyed very good business. But, with the infuence of the Court, heavy drinking had to take place outside. The Queen was abstemious – like all the Royal Family – but Edward, Prince of Wales, made a major change. He learned something about food and wine from his visits to France, and his gutsy enjoyment of them there was, later, to make the entertainment at Marlborough House – where the Prince and Princess of Wales then lived – of some influence. Bored with the drinking sessions that had been traditional after the ladies had left the table, the Prince, of a lively intelligence, wanted to join the ladies and to smoke a cigar, so traditions underwent a change. The variety of postprandial drinks was now not limited to port as the Prince enjoyed brandy.

FINGER GLASSES, FINGER BOWLS AND SOLITAIRES

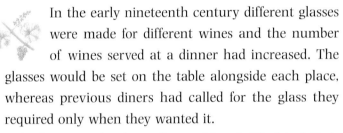 In the early nineteenth century different glasses were made for different wines and the number of wines served at a dinner had increased. The glasses would be set on the table alongside each place, whereas previous diners had called for the glass they required only when they wanted it.

At this time also (according to Maggie Black's *A Taste of History*, 1993) 'finger glasses' would be set on the table. These were used so that diners might rinse out their mouths before the sweet course, and although some visitors to Britain remarked on this being rather unpleasant to see at an otherwise smart dinner, they continued in use, though later tended to be used so that people could dip a corner of a napkin into the water and wipe both mouth and fingers. It was not long before the use of many foods that really did need to be eaten with the fingers necessitated the use of finger bowls, which would often have a flower or a large petal floating in them. The finger bowl eventually was set when the fruit was put before the diners. It has two lips, so that water may be poured off into a glass if required, but the fingers used for eating shellfish, nibbling the bones of cutlets, enjoying asparagus, can also be rinsed and dried in a napkin – the polite host would provide separate napkins after the finger bowls were cleared away with any debris therein.

Another type of glass, seldom seen nowadays, does appear in antique shops, but is often mistaken for a finger bowl. This is the 'solitaire'. It has a lip on one side of the rim; on this the stem of a wine glass might be propped so that the bowl of the glass might be rinsed in the water. This enabled a single glass to be in use when several wines were to be offered. It was, in fact, a personal version of the Monteith or wine cooler with its scalloped edge.

THE POSSET – AND ITS POTS
THE SYLLABUB – AND ITS GLASSES

 Posset is another drink neglected by wine writers, and, although it seems to be of unknown origin, the *Shorter Oxford Dictionary* describes it as 'hot milk, curdled with ale, wine or other liquor, often with sugar, spices etc. formerly drunk as a delicacy and as a remedy for colds.' The posset should not be confused with the syllabub, because the posset

A Lambeth Delftware posset pot, with lid to keep the contents warm and handles to facilitate sipping. (*Private collection/Bridgeman Art Library*)

was a hot drink, but the syllabub, even when it was enhanced with the preliminary tag 'syllabub under the cow', was always a cold liquid.

The posset pot seems to have been known and in use since the time of Queen Elizabeth I. Examples that survive are often like flat-footed tumblers, have two

Nineteenth-century English glasses for syllabub. (*Private collection/ Bridgeman Art Library*)

handles at the sides, and spouts in their sides 'to let out the posset ale', as a contemporary mentions. They look somewhat like the feeding bottles used by those who cannot easily direct liquid into their mouths from a glass or beaker. The curdled part of the posset would remain on top and be scooped off, but the dregs, which of course contained the succulent part of the mixture, were at the bottom. Syllabubs, which featured at noble tables, and might be in precious metal as well, were simpler to serve than possets because of being cold –

they could be served in small dishes or cups as well as in glasses.

There are also small glass cups with handles which seem to be what are termed 'custard cups'. This could signify that they held a thick rich sweet mix, but it is suggested by a world-famous authority, Richard Charleston, that they may be orgeat or lemonade glasses. Orgeat, according to the *Shorter Oxford Dictionary*, is 'a syrup or cooling drink made originally from barley, later from almonds and orange-flower water'.

All these mixes could be utilised by the household who might wish to provide a drink to guests but at the same time use up wines and spirits either already open or considered to be past their most enjoyable life.

REGIONAL GLASSES

Many of the European wine regions have evolved glasses that are supposed to be ideal for the local wines. Treviris glasses, from Trier, on the Moselle, are quite small, and the bowls are cut in a special pattern. They were obviously intended for the leisurely appraisal of the finest Moselle wines, sipped among a group of friends, with possibly only a slightly sweet biscuit or slice of sponge cake to go with them. The glasses of Vouvray are slightly convoluted, with a brim opening out, Alsace glasses often have a green stem and the use of tinted glasses that often filled the shelves of our great-grandparents were because people were shy of seeing 'bits' in wine when filtration hadn't always succeeded in removing them before bottling.

TOASTING GLASSES AND THE TOASTMASTER'S GLASS

In the seventeenth century English glassworks enjoyed great prestige and their bottles, as well as glasses, were much in demand. As fashionable people began to raise their glasses to drink the health of someone famous or loved, it became a habit to break the glass, so that no less worthy 'toast' should ever pollute the glass. Hence, millions of thin, fragile glasses, on stems, were produced; it is astonishing that so many have survived. There's a touching episode in one of Rudyard Kipling's stories about a man who, apparently lost for years, manages to find his way back to the original regiment from which enemies had abducted him. No one can work out who he is, although some clues are given. Then, having sat the man at table with a glass before him, the Colonel repeats the Loyal Toast and the strange man rises and says 'The Queen, God bless her!' and as he does so, he drinks and snaps the stem of the glass between his fingers. This establishes who he is – an officer.

Yet glassware couldn't always be crashing to the floor and there was one glass that certainly could not. This was the toastmaster's glass. It is on a stem, but has a thick bowl and foot and is rather small in capacity. This was so that the toastmaster could bang on the table with the glass to silence diners and to bring them to their feet with the announcement as to whom they were drinking; the toastmaster himself obviously couldn't drink much on such occasions, so that his glass never held more than a scant mouthful.

JACOBITE GLASSES

 Engraved glasses commemorate many people and events. The Jacobite glasses, with the outline of the Old or the Young Pretender and some even bearing the profile of King William (of Orange) may be seen in museums. To express allegiance to the Stuarts was easy – those who adhered to that cause drank claret and, when possible, they would pass their glass over the water jug or a Monteith or cooler to signify that they were expressing their

A selection of Jacobite drinking glasses. Some bear the white rose of Bonnie Prince Charlie. (*The Drambuie Collection, Edinburgh/Bridgeman Art Library*)

loyalty to the King 'over the water'. Some wine glasses were engraved with the white rose, the word 'Amen' or 'Fiat' – all Jacobite signs.

THE COPITA

This glass is traditionally associated with sherry. It is on a short stem, with a bowl that is incurving but of a moderate size. The stem of the glass can be held between the fingers while the wine is swirled within the glass. There are of course different sizes of copitas, but sherry should never be served in a thimble-sized vessel, nor should it ever be poured so that the drinker cannot swirl it around in the glass and sniff. It is significant that sherry is a wine that those who love it enjoy drinking as fresh as possible – with fino, manzanilla or any decent dryish sherry the bottle should go into the refrigerator when people have had enough. Ideally, *aficionados* opt for drinking sherry either off the bottling line or, if possible, when the *capataz* has drawn a sample from the cask.

THE ELGIN GLASS

The Elgin is an ill-proportioned glass, unsuited for the drinking of anything except something medicinal when one is desperate – such as the caudle, a hot spiced drink, made with wine and gruel, and the sort of thing medical men of previous centuries would suggest to soothe feverish patients. It is on a short stem whose bowl curves upward and outwards. The name comes – no one is quite sure why – from the title of the Lord Elgin (1766–1841) who negotiated the removal of the marbles that are associated with his name from the Parthenon in

Athens and about which endless arguments persist as to whether they should be returned to Greece.

It is said that this Lord Elgin was a parsimonious man, so had a glass designed for him that should give a mean measure. However, the factor of the present Lord Elgin was able to assure me, after perusing all relevant papers, that this is not so. He agreed that the glass is ungainly and unsuitable – and the larger size, known as the 'schooner' is even worse! These unsatisfactory glasses are not often seen nowadays and any sensible lover of wine will reject them should they be served.

TASTING CUPS

Anyone invited into the tasting room of those engaged in wine in Europe may see one or two shallow silver cups arranged or displayed. These are not – as has occasionally been thought – ashtrays! They are the tasting cups that, until quite recently, were carried by members of the wine trade so as to be sure of being able to taste from something familiar – rather than a possibly grubby glass, or pottery vessel. They are metal, to avoid the risk of being broken when travelling, have a loop or ring through which a ribbon or cord might pass so that the owner does not risk losing the tasting cup by putting it down and forgetting to pick it up.

There are a number of different kinds and in the days of local craftsmen, tasting cups of specific regions were marked with the devices of the area on the outside.

The most famous is probably the Burgundy *tastevin*, shallow, with a thumb piece to hold at one side, with indentations and stridulations inside: when a sample of wine had been poured into the *tastevin*, it could have been tilted so that the wine ran over the indentations, displaying its colour, for Burgundy cellars might be underground and dark. It is this type of *tastevin* it that many head sommeliers wear on a ribbon around their necks as, although they may not use it when serving wine these days, it became traditional so that they

A *tastevin* made in the typical Burgundian style and traditionally worn around the neck of the head sommelier. (*Birchgrove Products Ltd, Guildford*)

could sample a wine as they served it by means of pouring a small amount into their *tastevin*.

There are many variations in the shape of this type of vessel, but most members of the wine trade carried them. The *tastevin* that belonged to the great Madame Clicquot is very small – it could have been slipped into a pocket or reticule. The Bordeaux *tasse à vin* is slightly different. Because wine is usually kept above ground in the chais of Bordeaux, the limpidity of the wine is all that is important. So the *tasse à vin* is like a small steep-sided saucer, with a bulge in the middle – very plain. The type of sampling cup used in some lodges in Gaia, centre of the port trade, is a *tomboladero*: it is a largish saucer, with a bulge in the middle, but no indentations or decorations around. The point of this is that the young wine had to be examined in a bright light, showing its shades as it was tipped over the central bulge.

It is fair to say that the use of such specialised tasting cups is on the wane these days, as the tasting rooms where wines are seriously appraised will now be brightly lit and, even if they are not, additional lighting, of the least flattering kind, will have been installed.

SIX

ALL IN THE NAME

WELL, WHAT *IS* IN A NAME?

The names of wine estates, vineyards or plantations of vines may sometimes seem banal to wine lovers who hope for historic associations, family traditions and picturesque folklore. But this is unfair. Think of the banality of the names of many otherwise pleasant houses! There are also the names of owners, even from long ago, that have remained attached to properties and in use. And there is the way in which, with time, the name may have altered, either because people found it difficult to pronounce the original name or because some tag or word became attached to the produce of that place and was found to be a useful way of promoting sales. This happened with Pontac (see pp. 44–5). Those who enjoy Chambertin, Napoleon's supposedly favourite tipple, may, nowadays, be unaware of the tale that, once, the vineyard belonged to a man called Bertin – hence, it was the *champ* (field) of Bertin. It is also said that, after one very successful vintage, Monsieur Bertin loaded up a cask of his wine which he wished to present to the King; he got himself and his cask up to Paris and attended the Mass at which the monarch would be present – but Bertin was a very tall man and, when he seemed to lack respect by not kneeling down, shocked guards came to deal with him. However, they found

Picking grapes below the Château de Saumur on the Loire,
from the *Très Riches Heures du Duc de Berry*. (*Musée Condé,
France/Bridgeman Giraudon*)

that he *was* on his knees, but even so he towered above
the rest of the congregation. The King enjoyed the
wine – and Bertin presumably did good business
thereafter. Then there is Montrachet. This can be a
superlative white Burgundy. But do those who enjoy it
know – or, frankly, care – that the name comes from
the Latin, *Mons arachiensis*, meaning the mountain
from which the trees have been pulled up? (Incidentally,

the 't' in the middle of the word is not sounded if you are speaking French.)

In many famous sites in Germany the associations with religious establishments of the past are retained. But the influence of those who attempted to gain publicity and sales for a type of German wine caused the creation of Liebfraumilch, which, in the Depression between the two World Wars, was certainly a good idea. Originally, the name was applied to the wines grown from the vines produced within the vineyards belonging to the Liebfrauenstift (the Church of Our Lady) in Worms. This is very pleasant, but it is not a vineyard famous for great quality wines. Today, the term, according to the German Wine Law, is applied to strictly controlled wines that may come from other regions.

Within Europe, there are also clashes by properties that have managed to retain their independent operations, existing side by side with those under state control. Hungary is one of these. So, in a smaller way, is Cyprus, where the great wineries in Limassol produce wines to please the general public, but which, alas, may often lack the individuality of those made by properties belonging to religious holdings. Obviously, one should not appraise any wine because it has a charming name or has historic associations, but they do appeal to many novice drinkers. Background information seems paltry or difficult to read on many labels.

The Bordeaux Region

Because of the 299 years when the English crown owned this section of France, there are many names that seem to be related to English history – although not always reliably. Château Montrose, for example, is nothing to do with the great Marquis of that name, but acquired the tag because at certain times in the year the heather, which once covered the vineyard, would bloom and look pink. Similarly, Château Talbot does not seem to have any association with the great Earl of Shrewsbury, John Talbot, who was defeated at the Battle of Castillon; this may have been the first instance of artillery, brought up by Joan of Arc's companion-in-arms, Dunois, proving too much for old-fashioned chivalry. Château Beychevelle is said to be where passing ships had to strike their sails in salute to the Grand Admiral of France, who lived there, but Clive Coates, MW, relates in *Grands Vins* (1995) that it is doubtful whether the Grand Admiral ever did live there; the place may have been where the local authorities could check the cargoes and exact taxes on the passing vessels.

In the Graves (see my *Wines of the Graves*, 1988), where wine was being made when the Médoc was mostly a swamp, one great property is that of Pape Clément. This really did belong to a Pope. The de Goth family of Gascony were powerful in the area and Bertrand de Goth was given the estate by one of his brothers, as it provided a pleasant resort near Bordeaux. Bertrand de Goth came much under the influence of the King of France, who coveted the wealth of the great Order of the Knights Templars. The then head of the Templars – Temple station in London is named after one of their establishments – was summoned to France and burned at the stake; dying, he pronounced doom on both the King and the Pope – Clément V, the former Bertrand de Goth. Pope Clément V became ill and in fact both he and the king died in the same year, 1314. His tomb is in the quiet little church at Uzeste where he wished to be buried, and, during the Wars of Religion, it was looted. The wine of the estate Pape Clément, after various vicissitudes, continues to be fine and the crossed keys of St Peter and the triple tiara, formerly worn by Popes, still feature on its labels.

Two beautiful Médoc estates are those of Langoa and Léoville Barton. The first Thomas Barton came from an Irish Protestant family arriving in Bordeaux in 1722; the family flourished and even at one time hoped to acquire Château Lafite. Langoa was purchased in 1821 and various adjacent portions of vineyard were subsequently acquired. During World War II the late Ronald Barton, who went off to join the British army, was able to rely on his colleagues, including the Guestiers, with whom his family had become associated, to convince the Germans that as the property belonged to Ireland they had no right to it, although some German officers were billeted in the château. Léoville is very attractive and Ronald Barton's nephew, Anthony, maintains the property, where the wines invariably command respect.

Château Palmer is one of the picturesque properties along the Route des Châteaux in the Médoc; at one time it belonged to another Gascon family, the de Gasqs, also to the Ségur family. The Palmers, a west of England family, are somewhat difficult to sort out, but Charles Palmer, then in the 10th Dragoons, a chic regiment, travelled up to Paris in the same carriage as a lady who

The back of the Château Palmer on the Route des Châteaux. (*Mick Rock/Cephas*)

had decided to sell the estate – which is when Charles Palmer gave the property his name. He attempted many transformations, but was unlucky when he asked 'Prinny', the Prince Regent, later George IV, to sample some of the wines. Unfortunately the Prince was then accompanied by Lord Yarmouth, a man who is said to have been the model for Thackeray's wicked Lord Steyne in *Vanity Fair*. Yarmouth opted for the brew then being sold in London by a fashionable caterer and there was nearly a duel between the two men. Poor Palmer, discouraged, pulled up many of his vines. The 'P' that visitors see in various places on the château today is the initial of the Pereire banking family, who subsequently bought the estate. But Palmer has had a lasting influence on the British wine trade since the middle of the nineteenth century and many of the young men who have gone on to head firms and influence many trends in the UK wine business began by doing a 'stage' or session, making the vintage or studying at Palmer, now largely owned by the firm of Sichel.

The New World and the Cape
In the New World wine estates or firms tend to take the name of those who started them, or else they may be named for the nearest town. In South America properties often have picturesque names. But the Cape vineyards, in South Africa, are of importance because

not only does the history of wine here date from 1659, but the use of two languages – Afrikaans and English – provides an atmospheric tag to many historic properties.

At Tulbagh there is the Twee Jongegezellen estate; the Krone family are able to trace their ownership back for over a century – and before that they were in the wine and spirit business there. A poignant name is that of Allesverloren, in the Swartland. This has been under vines since 1704 and the Malan family, who have owned it since 1872, are one of the Cape's most important wine dynasties. The name derives from the time when the then owners left to attend a church service that was being held nearby; this was a major event for the earlier families and an occasion for great sociability. But when the owners of the estate returned they looked down from the mountains that surround the property and saw that the local bushmen had come down, burned the house and farm and driven off the animals. 'All is lost', commented the owner. But he rebuilt the estate which is of great importance today.

Kanonkop, in Stellenbosch, gets its name because, years ago, there used to be a cannon that was placed on the top of the adjacent mountain, from where a look-out could see when a ship was entering the harbour at Cape Town. The firing of the cannon signified the arrival and people would harness their vehicles to go into market and do business.

One Cape wine that may deserve a little explanation is the Rubicon of Meerlust. This beautiful property has been in the hands of the Myburgh family for more than two centuries but, in 1980, the late Nico Myburgh, with his renowned wine maker, Giorgio, launched, as my friend Michael Fridjhon says, 'one of the first Cabernet/Merlot blends to be marketed in the Cape'. Up to that time mixes of grape varieties were rather disdained and couldn't be given 'superior status' rating. Rubicon changed all that and its achievements have won it a great reputation. (The name, incidentally, comes from the little river that divides Italy from transalpine Gaul; when Julius Caesar crossed it in 49 BC he brought his army into Italy – establishing himself as an invader. So 'crossing the Rubicon' has come to mean taking a decisive step.)

Constantia is the wine name that kept Cape wines' reputation for at least two hundred years. The remarkable Simon van der Stel acquired the entire region in 1685 – he knew how the mountains would shield the pastures, how the sea breezes would ventilate the whole area. In fact, although most Cape wine regions are both beautiful and well sited, Constantia is breathtakingly wonderful – and an admirable site for vineyards. The whole property passed through several hands, however, until 1778, when it was bought by Hendrik Cloete. In 1823 the region was divided again and the fame of both red and white Constantia wine was known throughout Europe and in North America – although many of those who bought 'Constantia' probably didn't get the real thing. There were several changes of direction in the nineteenth century, but in 1976 the main estate was taken over, together with one of the adjoining farms; it was then developed as a tourist attraction and in spite of serious problems, including a fire in the historic house, the estate has been very well developed. The original cellar – the exuberant decorations on this shocked the locals when it was first built – is now an important wine museum and the vineyard has been put in order, although it must be said that the site of 'Lady Anne Barnard's bath' is probably nothing to do with her. At Klein Constantia, nearby, the estate is now very fine with a notable winery, admirably equipped for receiving visitors.

But the mystery is – who was Constance? She wasn't van der Stel's wife, she seems to have had no connection with him or his associates. Maybe the name 'Constance' is just a memory that van der Stel wished to commemorate.

Australasia

It would be unwise even to attempt to generalise about the wines of this vast continent. A range of their wines feature in all general wine lists of the United Nations, but it is fair to say that some of the very finest are snapped up locally as soon as available – and cost a lot even in their homelands. If in search of information, the library at Australia House in London, and New Zealand House likewise, can usually be helpful. But the situation changes all the time; until quite recently wine was not made, or at least not commercially, in Tasmania. Now a small quantity is. Everywhere there are new vineyards where, thanks to modern technology, wines that are good, sometimes very good indeed, are being produced. All should be tried when possible, and the big brands and inexpensive wines now exported in quantity should not be taken as wholly typical of the various countries, within which there are varied soils and climates and where progressive winemakers are annually challenged to make experiments and evolve innovative wines. Although export markets are considered important, it's the local demand on which many of the producers depend.

The wine contests make front page news in the newspapers and attract the same sort of publicity that is devoted to sporting events in the UK. The wine schools and the departments of oenology at the universities are widely respected: graduates from Roseworthy and Wagga, for example, have the big firms waiting for them. There's no snobbishness about qualifications in wine, and many of those influential in Australasia today did some studies in both Europe and the USA.

This is all the more fascinating because, in the earliest days, it was usually the doctors on the ships that carried the 'undesirables' out to Australia who founded the wineries, so that the names of many are retained in the titles of today's major firms. It is even said that one young doctor was so anxious to explore the new continent in the nineteenth century that he committed some minor crime so as to get himself included in the shipload of those being transported! It was the missionaries who came to New Zealand, with their families, whereas Australia tended to be more of a man's realm in earlier days.

In 'the land of the long white cloud', the Maori name for New Zealand, the wines can show a certain freshness plus fruit. But they come in a huge variety these days and the vineyards are extending. This is also true of virtually all the Australian vineyards, for the knowledge of controlling fermentation has made it possible to make wines capable of lasting throughout being transported – so that the days when Anthony Trollope praised wines in the vineyards that, later, disappointed him because of lack of care during shipping, are long gone.

WINE LABELS

 Before there was a great range of wines available – and, certainly, before drinkers became aware of the status symbol a choice bottle might contain – bottles of wine were more casually labelled. A customer would buy so many dozen from his merchant and he might even have his own bottles into which wine would be put, sometimes with a device or seal on the bottle. Yet, as wine drinking became more choice, labels were hung round the bottles, indicative of the contents. Some of these bottle labels, which were also looped around the neck of decanters, are very finely crafted and there is a fine exhibition of

Madeira wine labels to hang on decanters. (*Private collection/ Bridgeman Art Library*)

them in the entrance to Vintners' Hall, in the City of London. But the thing that can puzzle viewers is the way in which some names are strange: what is 'Tinto', 'Mountain', 'Buda', 'Reres', 'Calcavella'?

In some instances, the craftsmen employed to make the bottle labels were not English-speaking, and they may not have had instructions in writing as to what was to be put on the bottle labels. 'Sherry' is easy enough – but 'Xeres' is what the silversmith may have understood. 'Tinto' obviously indicates a red wine, but 'Mountain' might have indicated a superior growth from higher up the vineyard. 'Indian sherry' referred to such wines as had been sent as ballast in vessels going from the East Indies via the Cape of Good Hope – the long sea voyage improving and softening the wine. Some labels indicate quality: 'best claret', 'F claret', 'Old Claret', 'premier claret', 'dinner claret' and even 'after dinner claret'. To this day, however, the label – or bottle label – may not always be a guarantee of origin.

DAVIS

A casual reference to someone having studied at Davis should win respect – for this is the world-famous department of oenology at the University of California. Although it is fair to say that not everyone at Davis knows everything about wine, they still enjoy not only a great reputation but their resources are considerable. All students of wine owe a debt to Davis – even if sometimes they may not agree with the promulgations emanating from that respected establishment.

SEKT

This term is German and is used to signify sparkling wine. Its origin is obscure but it is thought that, at the beginning of the nineteenth century, the actor Ludwig Devrient, famous for his interpretation of Shakespearean parts, notably Falstaff, would often call for 'A cup of sack!' when he wanted a drink; as his favourite drink was Champagne he may often have had to put up with other sparkling wines, but the use of the term caught on.

HOCK

Many suppose that this term, used to designate the wines of Germany in general, started in the nineteenth century, when the town of Hochheim, on the River Main which runs into the Rhine, is supposed to have been a favourite of Queen

Victoria. The queen actually gave her name to the Viktoriaberg site. The earliest use of the word 'hock' seems to have been an anglicized version of the word 'hockamore', an English version of Hochheim, for which the *Shorter Oxford Dictionary* gives the earliest use way back in 1625. The term 'Rhenish' for Rhine wines was certainly in use in the nineteenth century.

PUNCH

This word – not included in many dictionaries of wine – is of considerable interest. It is found in many recipe books up to World War II, and in America even since then, and many famous restaurants have their 'special' types of punch, which, it is supposed, are used for parties and gatherings of various types. It seems never to have featured in British or European eating-places in recent times, although sometimes versions of it are put together for mixed social gatherings, such as may be arranged for fundraising purposes.

According to *The Diner's Dictionary* by John Ayto (1993), it was officers of the East India Company who brought punch back to England in the early part of the seventeenth century. As will be appreciated, various ways of making imported wines and spirits palatable after being opened were useful. Ayto makes the interesting point that mixes that do not contain either citrus fruits or spices should be properly termed 'cups', but this is a topic that drinkers may find something to argue about. He also states that the original Hindi word would have been pronounced with a 'short "oo" sound', and he thinks there may have been some possibility of the word deriving from 'puncheon', a large cask, from which such mixes might have been drawn off. In 1698 John Fryer asserted in his book *Account of East India* that the word 'punch' came from a Hindi word *'panch'*, signifying 'five', because of the five ingredients – sugar, spices, lemon or lime juice, spirits and water. But this recipe was too simple to appeal to diners-out who aspired to smartness and all sorts of other ingredients were soon involved, including some for the composition of a non-alcoholic version, such as punch made with the chic drink, tea.

It is important to remember that, even in Europe at this period, many sources of water might be suspect and some sort of mouthwash was useful before wines were consumed in the course of a meal and, as something chilled was highly acceptable, the punch recipe came into widespread use.

From surviving recipes punch seems to have been made either hot or cold. It is interesting that, in some accounts of serious drinkers of wine, this was

Modern Midnight Conversation, circle of William Hogarth, showing the punch bowl in use. (*Phillips Auctioneers, UK/Bridgeman Art Library*)

undertaken outside the context of a meal so that the casual mixed drink was really something to provide hospitality while more serious wine was prepared.

From the recipes involved, it would seem that 'punch' was also often served during a meal – hence the large and often elaborate punch bowls, now often beautiful antiques and sometimes mistaken for wine coolers – and might have been a way of using up dregs of wine from the decanters; and anything that wasn't pleasant by itself to drink could be rendered acceptable in a well-adjusted mixture.

It is wise to bear in mind that there is usually a reaction from any type of prohibition or excess of food and drink, so that, although Oliver Cromwell was not a total abstainer, it was to be expected that the restoration of Charles II, who had spent much of his life in Europe, would encourage wine consumption on a more lavish scale than had existed under the Common-wealth. Various types of 'punch' proliferated and, at a time when many went across the Atlantic for religious or political reasons, the use of mixed drinks went with them. It is interesting that it does not seem to have gone in more than a few instances to the southern hemisphere. Regions in which vines could be grown – and wine made – from the late seventeenth century in South Africa and, subsequently, in Australasia, either had plenty of wine available or else they opted for some form of spirit.

AN HEROIC TIPPLE

For many years the casual drink in Burgundy and, increasingly, its environs, has been *vin blanc cassis* – the white wine of the region, perked up with a few drops of Cassis (blackcurrant) liqueur. For purists, the wine should be Bourgogne Aligoté. But, with the usefulness of this drink in many regions, it began, even before World War II, to lose its wholly Burgundian associations – any dryish white wine would do.

In World War II, however, the French Resistance in the region was inspired by a tiny man, Canon Félix Kir, Mayor of Dijon. He was fearless and when, with others of the Resistance, he faced a firing squad of Germans, he somehow avoided the bullets and then ran furiously towards the soldiers who, understandably terrified, fled from him. Since that time the Burgundian drink has been named 'un Kir' in his honour.

A small problem arose when, some years ago, the then President of the USSR visited France and was going to visit Burgundy. Tact was required to deal with the naming of another local drink, even more so because, in the jovial Beaujolais, a dollop of Cassis liqueur into a glass of the red wine of the region was known as a '*rince cochon*' – pigswill. How could the guest be invited to sample such a drink? The solution was to name it for the visitor – 'un Nikita'. But I don't suppose many barmen in Burgundy would have remembered this for long!

The important thing about making this drink is that the white wine should have a certain amount of acidity; the mix made with Riesling, for example, always seems somewhat disappointing. If a dryish sparkling wine is used, then the mixture becomes a 'Kir royale'.

LADIES' CHAIN

It may surprise many to know that the retail chain named 'Victoria Wine' after the great queen herself was originally established so that respectable women could go and buy wines without having to jostle their way into public houses. Only ladies were employed and they were subject to quite strict regulations about black dresses, discreet hair styles and no jewellery except for a wedding ring. Not only did these splendid ladies run the shops at the outset of this venture in the nineteenth century, but they also did the cellarwork and were truly informed about wine. For small-scale deliveries they would use a hand cart, although for large amounts of wine it was necessary to make use of men and boys.

'Vic Wine', as it was familiarly known, was a valued source of supply to many people and it was only in recent years that one of the big firms in the British wine trade bought it. Unfortunately the archives of the firm were mostly destroyed in World War II, but the fact that ladies ran the shops with obvious success is indicative of the way in which their sex was no obstacle to their so doing.

SEVEN

TOASTS AND TRADITIONS

'TOAST' AND THE LADY OF BATH

 This word does not seem to have been included in many reference books about wine. Yet its origin may be of interest. In medieval times, before wine was bottled to keep it in condition, those who kept inns, taverns and similar places where drink was on sale might find, towards the end of a cask's contents, that the wine was poor in flavour. Then the innkeeper would float on the surface of the drink a piece of bread – the substantial hand-baked type – that had been held before the fire and then rubbed with a spice such as cinnamon, ginger, or some herb that would provide extra flavour and draw attention away from the rather dreary liquid in the beaker. In the months before the new wine was shipped this 'little extra' was much appreciated. Shakespeare's Falstaff asks for 'a quart of sack; put a toast in't'.

Richard Steele, however, wrote in *The Tatler*, in 1709:

this term had its rise in the town of Bath in the reign of Charles the Second. It occurred that a celebrated beauty of the time was bathing in the Cross Baths, and one of her admirers took a glass of the water in which the fair one stood and drank her health to the company. There was in the place a gay fellow, half fuddled, who offered to jump in, and swore, although he liked not the liquor, he would have the toast. He was opposed in his revolution yet this whim gave foundation to the present honour which is given to the lady we mention in our liquors, who has ever since been called a toast.

This is related in a charming book *Hogmanay and Tiffany* by Gillian Edward (1970). Only a little later than Steele playwright Richard Brinsley Sheridan (1751–1816) indicates in *The School for Scandal* that the word 'toast' could signify acclaim of either an individual or a cause. The drinking song in this play runs:

> Here's to the maiden of bashful fifteen;–
> Here's to the widow of fifty;–
> Here's to the flaunting extravagant quean [a tart]
> And here's to the housewife that's thrifty.
> Let the toast pass –
> Drink to the lass,
> I'll warrant she'll prove an excuse for the glass.

The association of a 'toast' with a particular cause or an individual – as with the head of state – is also something that is 'honoured', in usually informal ways, when someone has a birthday or at a wedding. There is a long tradition behind the way in which wines are drunk in Britain; Fynes Morrison writes in his *Itinerary*, in 1617: 'For the point of drinking, the English at the

Sir William Quiller Orchardson's *The Young Duke, c.* 1889, showing the company toasting him at a grand dinner. (*The Fine Art Society/Bridgeman Art Library*)

feast will drink two or three healths in remembrance of special friends, or respectful honourable persons.'

The original type of 'toast', with extra flavour being given to a drink by means of herbs, spices or extra liquors may never be revived. Today's skilful barman will perk up a slightly flat drink in many ways. But it was the lady in Bath who made toasts chic.

TWO EXCEPTIONS TO TRADITION

 There are two exceptions to the tradition of the company standing up to honour the Loyal Toast to the sovereign. The first is when this is proposed aboard ship. There are two tales about why the company should then remain seated, one saying that the custom originated under William IV (the 'Sailor King'), who bumped his head when he stood up, the other being about 'Prinny', later George IV, who felt seasick.

Others who do not stand up on this occasion are the Benchers of Lincoln's Inn, that historic hall in which *Twelfth Night* was first produced. But it was in the time of Charles II that the entire company were so merry that few if any of them could actually rise to their feet – at which the King gave permission for the toast to be drunk while all were seated.

SMOKING AND THE LOYAL TOAST

At many formal functions, luncheon as well as dinner, the toastmaster will usually announce that the company may rise to stand and thereby honour the sovereign. It is general, nowadays, to follow this, after people have seated themselves, with the announcement that they may now smoke. It is odd to know that, in the 1890s, a book on dining actually advocated the pause for a cigarette, although it may have been referring exclusively to dinners for men only. Even prior to World War II diners might be offered the choice of either an Egyptian or a Russian cigarette in the interval between the principal course of the meal so as to change the palate.

There was one awkward moment, post-World War II but within the memory of many, when, at a dinner at the Savoy Hotel, London, the gorgeous Marlene Dietrich lit a cigarette during the meal. Those present seemed to find her amused that anyone objected. In table settings of the late Duke and Duchess of Windsor, ashtrays were set on the table at each place. A curious variation on this occurred when an important guest, obliged to leave early to attend some essential meeting or conference, made the toastmaster announce the Loyal Toast at the end of the first course of the meal! In some countries, of course, smoking during the meal doesn't interfere with the enjoyment of the food and wines. Or so the locals suppose.

THE STIRRUP CUP AND THE BON ALLAY

This is a drink traditionally served to members of a hunt before they move off and, consequently, it has become associated with the 'one for the road' drink which many hosts offer guests, or, as a gentle hint, try to get them to leave. The stirrup cup was once offered to those who couldn't alight from

Major Edward Bonner-Maurice, MFH Tanatside Hunt, enjoying a stirrup cup at a Boxing Day meet in Welshpool, Powys. (*Jim Meads*)

their horses or get down from the carriages, so that the drink had to be sipped or quaffed where they were. The traditional glass could not be stood down as it had no foot; as the glass was emptied, it had to be turned upside down on the tray of the servant.

The Bon Allay is a version of the stirrup cup and was known to be the drink to speed the parting guest.

THE LOVING CUP

According to Chambers' *Book of Days*, the ceremony of the Loving Cup, which is traditional with all Livery Companies, is said to date

The Vintners' loving cup, *c.* 1745–6. This is what would have been used at a City banquet. It is quite heavy to hold and the person drinking would certainly have been unable to resist a sudden attack. The Distillers' Company put a dagger on the table as an additional precaution. (*The Vintners' Company*)

back before the Norman Conquest of 1066, and to derive from the assassination, by command of Elfrida, of King Edward while drinking.

It was customary with our Anglo-Saxon forefathers, in drinking parties, to pass round a large cup, from which each drank in turn to some of the company. He who thus drank stood up, and, as he lifted the cup with both hands, his body was exposed without any defence to a blow, and the occasion was often seized by an enemy to murder him. When one of the company stood up to drink, he required the companion who sat next to him, or some of the party, to be his pledge, and his companion, if he consented, stood up also and raised his drawn sword in his hand to defend him while drinking.

Nowadays, the cup passes round the table, each guest drinking to his neighbour. When the guest about to drink a Loving Cup stands up, those on either side of him also rise. The guest on one side stands with his back to the one who is about to drink to as to protect him from attack. The latter and the guest on his side bow to each other, the second guest removes the cover, the first guest drinks, and wipes the rim of the cup with the napkin provided, the second guest replaces the cover and the two bow to each other again. The same procedure is followed by the second guest with his next neighbour, the first guest meantime mounting guard, and the one who has been protecting him sits down again.

It is believed that the Distillers' Company is the only Livery Company to circulate daggers (symbolic with the sword referred to above) with the Loving Cup.

'No Heeltaps'

The odd word 'heeltap' seems to have come into the vocabulary of drinking speech because it became used for the draining of the wine that might remain in the bottom of a glass. In former times people of short stature were often wishful to increase their height and stature by adding a few inches to their heels or to the thickness of their shoes. In the eighteenth century the term for the bottom of the glass began to be used to refer to the drainings of the wine at its base. Before filtration was understood and regulated there might be much deposit at the bottom of a glass.

The exhortation 'No heeltaps' at the time of giving a toast, meant that the contents of the glass were to be completely drained. It is rare these days for a 'heeltap glass' to be available, but the exhortation 'No heeltaps!' still means the same.

THE ORIGIN OF 'GOOD HEALTH'

The act of wishing 'health' to the reigning sovereign is ancient. Beowulf strides into Hrothgar's hall to wish him 'Waes hael!' confident that he will be able to deal with the monster Grendel or, worse, Grendel's mother who prowls about at night and kills the warriors. But the wishing of 'health' is interesting: in former times, when life was cheap or pestilences raged, it was a more precious wish than today.

It is significant, also, that those who have offered food and drink to someone, even an enemy, keep that person safe until he has left their area – or the marked out region beyond their habitation. It is also significant that although food, even of a primitive kind, might be offered to a stranger, the most precious commodity was drink – water most of all. People can last a long time without food, without water they die soon.

PASSING THE PORT

Customs associated with port mean the use of vintage port. This is usually the last wine of a formal dinner, served after the 'ladies' have left the table and the men, as Lord Melbourne once remarked 'can talk broad!' It is unlikely that, today, chamberpots might appear or footmen to loosen the neckcloths of those diners who have drunk too much. Sideboards, then, as the dictionary explains, were designed not only to contain cutlery, linen and silver, but to contain the chamberpots when the gentlemen got down to serious after-dinner drinking.

The routine is that the cloth is cleared – *desservi* – so that 'dessert' consisting of fruit and nuts can be set on the polished board; then the decanter of port is placed in front of the host, who pours himself a helping and then passes the decanter, clockwise, to his left. When a guest of honour sits at the host's right hand, the host is allowed a 'backhander', by helping this person, and the action can be elegant, if the host rests the decanter or bottle along his forearm to pour. The port then goes around the table. It is thought that the way it circulates is either according to the circulation of the planets or else that to send it the other way round is bad luck – anti-clockwise or 'widdershins' was an action associated with black magic. If the port remains in front of anyone for an unreasonable time, it is the convention to ask 'Do you know the Bishop of Norwich?' supposedly because the original bearer of the title was a mean or unconvivial person, who would not pass on the port. Years ago there was a cleric who was a notorious bottle stopper, but it was somewhat surprising for one friend to receive the reply 'Yes, he's my godfather!'

But passing the port is a pleasant tradition and it may be of interest to know that, in the Factory House in Oporto, there are two dining-rooms: the diners – all men – rise and pass from one room to the other, so that no whiff of anything should affect the aroma and bouquet of the vintage port served in the adjoining room. As the men take their napkins with them, it has always seemed strange that these, retaining the smells of what has been eaten and drunk previously, are not replaced with clean linen.

EIGHT

HEROES AND HEROINES

Jefferson, the Statesman with the Corkscrew

Count Haraszthy and Buena Vista

Louis Pasteur and the Wine that gave Life and Health to Millions

Men of Port: the Abbot of Llamego and Baron J.J. Forrester

Negus

Chaptal

The Lady who did the Treading

Pioneering Women and the Champagne *Grandes Dames*

A Cape Lady and a Wine Snob

JEFFERSON, THE STATESMAN WITH THE CORKSCREW

 It would be hard to name any monarchs, heads of state or leaders of political parties who have been even vaguely knowledgeable about wine. How can they acquire any understanding of it with the hasty entertainments and irregular hours they have to keep? But there is one major exception: Thomas Jefferson (1743–1826), three times President of the United States, the man who drafted the Declaration of Independence whereby 'all men are created equal and independent', seems always to have been fascinated by the pleasures of the palate and, even as a law student, ordered wine in quantity.

When Jefferson was sent to France, just before the French Revolution, he was able to travel to wine regions in that country, as well as to Holland, Germany and Italy. He carried with him a small case that included a toothbrush, dentifrice, toothpicks, combs, pen, ink, paper and a corkscrew. In James M. Gabler's admirable *Passions: The Wines and Travels of Thomas Jefferson* (1995), this remarkable man's comments on vines, grapes and soils, additional to wines, are meticulously recorded. Of course, he travelled in some style, but he would ride up to fifty miles daily, not disdaining hiring mules to get through a tricky route and also walking. Edward Dunbauld's *Thomas Jefferson, American Tourist* (1946), makes the reader wonder whether Jefferson had any time for official work at all! Unfortunately on his visit to England, where he was entertained by many of the owners of fine houses and gardens – from which he sent back seeds and cuttings – he didn't take to his reception at the Court of King George III; hardly surprising, because Jefferson had been criticising the British very recently. He was credited with being well educated but his opinion that 'There never was a poet north of the Alps and there never will be one' seems indicative of no knowledge of Shakespeare, Milton, or any other of the British, French and Spanish masters of verse and drama, whom he may not have had time to explore.

The lordly way in which he could travel is demonstrated when, inspecting the Canal du Midi in 1788, he sometimes 'dismounted my carriage from its wheels, placed it on the deck of a light bark, and was then towed on the Canal instead of on the post road'. If anything in the countryside aroused his interest he would get out and ride but 'when fatigued I take my seat in my carriage where, as much at ease as in my study, I read, write and observe. My carriage being of glass all round admits a full view of the varying scenes through which I am shifted.' Jefferson loved the Bordeaux wines and when, some years ago, a bottle of

1787 Lafite was discovered in a cellar in Paris, the fact that it not only bore the name 'Lafitte' [*sic*] but also the initial 'Th.J' made the price at Christie's auction soar to a record £105,000.

Throughout his travels Jefferson arranged with various merchants and makers to ship wines to him and in fact he later risked being criticized because of his preference for European wines. But his interest in America was firm although some of the wines he enjoyed seem to indicate that maybe his palate had changed. Jefferson's interest in the sweet wines of Europe was understandable at this period, before sugar became cheap and Chaptal signed the famous authoris-ation permitting the addition of sugar to the 'must' of certain wines. Jefferson appreciated the Muscats, enjoyed dry sherry, and in his homeland experimented with many local grape varieties; he became a friend of John Adlum, tagged as 'the father of American viticulture'.

Endlessly hospitable, whether in office or as a private citizen, Jefferson entertained lavishly for so many guests that he was obliged to go and stay himself at a nearby property when his house, Monticello, was full. He corresponded with a Monsieur de Bergasse in Marseilles, who, together with his son, says Gabler 'could duplicate the taste of any wine by blending the wines of Languedoc'. One doubts this – but whether

Thomas Jefferson (1743–1826), 3rd president of the United States, entertained lavishly at his house, Monticello. (*Bridgeman Giraudon*)

the great man lost his teeth and maybe found that his palate had altered when back home cannot be known.

He was certainly abstemious: 'My measure is a perfectly sober one of 3 or 4 glasses at dinner and not a drop at any other time.' Yet the refreshments served at his table were beer and cider, wine not being offered until 'the cloth was removed'. The wine, according to Gabler, 'was sent up by a double dumb waiter located on each side of the fireplace'. At this time, when the smart hour for dining was sliding lower than the fading of daylight in Britain, it would be interesting to know whether Jefferson's later sessions over wine were the equivalent of what was to become 'supper' in Britain. . . . But, being a widower, his guests were sometimes all men. Is it fanciful to suggest that the main meal, dinner, with its beer and cider, was the main evening meal, but that the sessions over the wines might come into the category of 'supper' – then beginning to be a late night meal in Britain, after the port had been circulated and the men had staggered upstairs to join the ladies?

The wine glasses said to have been used in the Jefferson household are stemmed glasses, of triangular shape as regards the bowl; today, we should use them for sparkling wines. But he was always looking to the future, as his last letter suggests, 'To see what we have seen, to taste the tasted, and at each return, less tasteful; cover our palates to decant another vintage.' He died on the fiftieth anniversary of the Declaration of Independence.

COUNT HARASZTHY AND BUENA VISTA

Agoston Haraszthy de Mokesa, a Hungarian, was born in 1812. His origins were certainly lowly but from time to time he assumed the title of 'Count' or, occasionally, 'Colonel'. He arrived in America, according to John N. Hutchison in *The Book of*

California Wine (1984), in 1840 and, in a flamboyant way, made an impact wherever he went. Eventually he sent for his family and children and their adventures and travels deserve a whole book. He planted vineyards, built a house and engaged in all kinds of business; but the most important, to wine lovers, was his purchase of property in Sonoma, where he established a winery that he named Buena Vista.

Haraszthy was no static personality. He promoted everything to do with local wines, not merely his own; he visited Europe, he studied grapes and wrote a book about the varieties, and encouraged one of his sons, Arpad, to attempt to produce sparkling wines. He never ceased to explore new ways of furthering the local wines and, although set back by a fire in their distillery, he pushed on.

He had intended to go to Nicaragua, undertaking yet more enterprises, but in 1869 he disappeared, supposedly drowned while trying to cross a flooded stream – in which there were alligators.

Haraszthy's achievement was notable in wine; he was interested in every aspect of it. Two of his sons married into a family which might have been supposed to be a rival concern. The name of Buena Vista is commemorated today – and wine of quality is still made on the old site. According to Leon D. Adams in *The Wines of America* (1985) after a newsman, Frank Bartholomew, bought the property 'they succeeded where Haraszthy failed' and made the wines both respected, and ultimately very big business.

LOUIS PASTEUR AND THE WINE THAT GAVE LIFE AND HEALTH TO MILLIONS

The Jura region of France is beautiful but, even today, not much known. The local wines are tagged with the saying that 'The more you drink, the straighter you will hold yourself,' although this is probably hopeful publicity. One, however, exhibits a curious phenomenon, when sometimes a furry-looking and quivering coating forms on the surface, although it can disappear from time to time. This coating is termed 'the veil' and it does not seem to occur in other wine regions of France.

In 1822 a very bright and percipient boy was born at Dôle. He was encouraged to

Louis Pasteur (1822–95), whose discoveries saved the life of millions. (*Private collection/Bridgeman Art Library*)

pursue studies in science; he became in demand to advise several firms, including the silk manufaturers of Lyons, who were suffering from a plague that attacked the silkworms. The young man went up in business to become a famous scientist, gaining international renown for his work in the curing of rabies, which could then kill animals and humans in vast numbers. And, always, he remembered the 'veil' that sometimes covered certain of the local wines – the result of bacterial action, which will affect the ultimate wine significantly. For this was Louis Pasteur (1822–95) whose researches on bacterial action enabled him to evolve vaccines that could defeat the infection of a rabid animal's bite and whose work resulted in the way in which, today, foods, drinks, surgical instruments and an infinite quantity of items can be prevented from harbouring infection, so that his very name is commemorated in the word 'pasteurisation'.

Pasteur's work aroused furious denunciations by many at the time, but he remained a devout member of the Roman Catholic church and, although a statue of him shows him injecting a child, he always preferred his staff at the laboratories to treat children with what, then, could be a painful injection. He visited London and was received like the celebrity he had become, but curiously he never went to the south of Spain, where certain types of sherry grow the 'flor' or 'flower', akin to the 'veil'. In wine, the use of pasteurisation can, in certain circumstances, be helpful, although in others it may render the wine lifeless.

Louis Pasteur died in 1895. He is one of the great men of wine – but he would not have been if he had not been born in Dôle, and able to observe the phenomenon of the 'veil' in Jura wines. Of all the gifts that wine has given to man, the knowledge of bacterial action, as revealed to Louis Pasteur, has certainly been of inestimable and everlasting value.

MEN OF PORT: THE ABBOT OF LLAMEGO AND BARON J.J. FORRESTER

Port is one of the great fortified wines of the world, yet port itself is something of a mystery.

In the eighteenth century, two youngsters from Liverpool, travelling in wine for their firms, discovered a particularly pleasant one made by the Abbot of Llamego. How could this be? The Abbot was obviously a wine maker of ability and admitted that his wine had received a dollop of the local brandy. The rest is history. But we still don't know the names of the young men!

J.J. Forrester was born in Hull in 1809. His work, maps and drawings are an extraordinary achievement, and he is one of the great personages of the wine

Baron Forrester (1809–62), who did so much for the port wine trade. (*Port Wine Institute*)

world. He went out to join his uncle's Portuguese firm, Offley Forrester, and achieved outstanding success. He quickly acquired fluency in Portuguese, also got to know the River Douro well, producing beautiful maps and making delightful watercolours. He was created a Baron by the King of Portugal and acquired many decorations from other countries. His charm and the respect in which he was held enabled him to keep on good terms with people who were furious competitors as regards trade.

In 1844 he tried to establish his love of 'natural' wines, which aroused furious arguments and although there are still various opinions as to how port should be fortified, there were many abuses and distortions of the wine which Forrester was able to influence and reform. Forrester, in photographs, looks both handsome and forceful and it is one of the tragedies of wine that he ended his life early. Together with Baroness Fladgate and Dona Antonia Adelaide Ferreira, he went to luncheon at Quinta da Vargellas. As they were returning down the Douro, in the Cachao de Vazleira – even now, with the river higher than it was at that time, the steep, black surrounding cliffs give a sinister atmosphere although one knows one is safe – their shallow-bottomed boat capsized in the ravine. The two ladies, wearing the crinolines of the time, were borne up by the air under their skirts and floated to safety to a nearby beach or sandbank; Forrester's body was not recovered. It is thought he may have been wearing a moneybelt and although his son was later informed that the body was found and robbed, reports seem vague.

Sarah Bradford's *The Englishman's Wine: the story of port* (1969) gives some information about this very great man and shows photographs, which makes many wine lovers regret that a fully documented biography is not as yet available.

NEGUS

This drink is named after a Colonel Francis Negus, who presumably concocted it while on service in the Army. It consists of port or sherry, plus sugar, spices and hot water. Colonel Negus died in 1732; the drink often features in historical novels of the eighteenth century.

CHAPTAL

Jean-Antoine Chaptal (1756–1832), Comte de Chanteloupe, has given his name to one of the most important methods whereby wine is made both popular and may be commercially successful.

Chaptal was trained as a doctor and was fortunate to inherit and marry into money. He held various important posts in the early part of the Napoleonic period and then, in 1800, he was appointed Minister of the Interior, in succession to Lucien Bonaparte. His career progressed most satisfactorily and, in 1802, he wrote a book, *L'Art de Faire le Vin*. It is important, at this stage, to understand that adding sugar to the fermenting must will, in a poor vintage when the grapes do not possess sufficient sugar within themselves, enable them to complete their fermentation and prove pleasant wines. Christopher Fielden, in an erudite study of Chaptal (*Christie's Wine Companion*, 1989), relates that the monks of Clos Vougeot, in Burgundy, added loaf sugar to the vats in which fermentation was taking place. It is possible that for centuries before those in charge of wine making utilized such sweetening agents as might be obtained – honey, grape syrup, manna, cassia or molasses. When the new wine was sought after, this may not have distorted the wine's character much, but as soon as the possibility of keeping wines in bottles was noted, then the condition of the wine when it was bottled was naturally of great importance.

At the turn of the eighteenth century, however, France, with Napoleon's armies to cope with, had to have some sweetening agents. Cane sugar, from the West Indies, was increasingly difficult to obtain, thanks to the British Navy. There was, however, plenty of sugar beet in France, with two small refineries outside Paris, at Passy, where Baron Delessert, known as '*le roi du sucre*' inspected the establishment with Chaptal. Napoleon was most impressed. Chaptal did not 'invent' the process of chaptalization, but he did sign the decree authorizing its use. Until very recently indeed, sugar would arrive even at a top-class grocer in blocks, from which lumps had to be cut off with tongs or knives; 'lump sugar' was not then cut up in little rectangles.

Chaptal died in 1832 and people have been arguing about the use of chaptalization ever since with certain wines. At one time Burgundy, both white and red, attracted most of the derogatory comments, because the Burgundy region is not large and the weather can be capricious. More recently, there was a violent argument about the use of the procedure in the Bordeaux area. Christopher Fielden is definite that 'in the Mediterranean basin, in California and Australia it is forbidden' and it seems quite unknown in South Africa. . . . But wine is intended to give pleasure and it is a commodity to sell and, these days, the amounts in which wine is sold is big business. So, in some northern vineyards a wine might be weak in constitution and feeble in flavour but even a small amount of a sweetening agent could render it both palatable and commercially appealing.

The important thing about chaptalization is that it should not distort the character of a wine that had, previously, been established as representative of its region or vineyard. The small but informed addition of a sweetening agent can make an extraordinary difference, but there should never be anything obvious about chaptalization. A wine maladroitly chaptalized will seem to leave a sticky film within the mouth and have a soggy flavour; and an experienced taster will sometimes pick up the presence of the beet sugar – a coarse, flat element seeming alien to the original wine.

THE LADY WHO DID THE TREADING

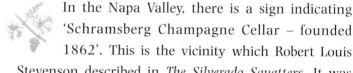In the Napa Valley, there is a sign indicating 'Schramsberg Champagne Cellar – founded 1862'. This is the vicinity which Robert Louis Stevenson described in *The Silverado Squatters*. It was Jacob and Annie Schram who entertained the Stevensons in 1880.

Jacob Schram arrived in 1842 and, being a barber from the Rhineland, tramped around the region working while his wife undertook the management of his vineyards. Schramsberg became very well known, its wines being listed in many chic hotels – even the Carlton Club in London.

Jamie Davies remains involved in the wine-making process and is a great ambassador for fine wine. (*Schramsberg Vineyards Company*)

Later, Jack L. Davies, of San Francisco, by various adroit business means, moved with his wife, Jamie, into the old Schram house. It was a gigantic task to get the old establishment into working order to suit present-day needs, but it was done – and, then, when the first grapes, in 1966, went into the crusher the machine broke down. Jamie Davies took off her shoes and went into the vat to assist the treading.

It is, of course, not permitted in Europe to use the term 'Champagne' for Schramsberg, but the wines bearing the name have achieved world fame. Jack Davies, unfortunately, is no longer with us, but the delightful Jamie is – and is a great ambassador for the fine wine, now made in a variety of styles.

PIONEERING WOMEN AND THE CHAMPAGNE *GRANDES DAMES*

It is still something that the ignorant remark – that any woman should be involved with wine. Yet for centuries they have been, in different ways. Even in England, in the Middle Ages, there was nothing to stop a woman from binding herself as an apprentice in the wine trade (and even in more unlikely guilds such as armourers, founderers, barber surgeons). Anne Crawford's *History of the Vintners' Company*

(1977) shows women could be extremely influential; when the menfolk were travelling about – possibly in foreign countries, selling or buying – the women often took an active part in London and, as widows, continued much of the charitable work they had pursued earlier. Joanna, widow of John Maykyn, herself left a substantial number of bequests. Alice Walworth, another vintner's widow, married yet another vintner and went to live in Chichester.

There were several women who kept firms going in later centuries, in Britain and abroad. In World War I, when for over a thousand days the population of Reims lived in the cellars under that city, the vineyards were tended by such elderly and young men who could creep out at night, while the cellarwork was done by the women.

More recently, the exotically beautiful Marimar Torres has transplanted herself to the USA from Catalonia, where the family name is internationally renowned. Marimar not only runs vineyards and makes wine, but writes books of delectable recipes! In Tuscany there is the delightful Contessa Guerrerie Rizzardi; she has been experimenting with the use of different woods for their headstaves of casks – what difference may they make to her usually crisp, zippy wine?

In the Cape of South Africa, women play a major part in wine education as well as production. Norma

Ratcliffe, wholly outside the wine world, came to the region to make wines of world renown. Her wines from Warwick Estate are both creative and worthy of comparison with any. Phyllis Hands, founder of the Cape Wine Academy, is only one of the teachers whose reputations have extended beyond their own country. And mention must be made of Louise Hofmeyer, daughter of a famous wine critic and maker, who, when her father became ill, continued his work with distinction.

Yet the best-known ladies of the wine world must be the delightful Champagne 'widows': Madame Pommery, who ran the business significantly; wise Madame Bollinger who was 'Tante Lily' to so many of the *champenois* and was the first woman to be invited to the great annual banquet of the UK Wine & Spirit Trade's function; and, more recently, the delicious Madame Odette Pol Roger, of whom Winston Churchill said that he could see 'the sparkles in her hair'.

But the truly '*Grande Dame*' of Champagne must be Madame Clicquot. She was actually married in a cellar because, during the French Revolution, her wise father, who was Mayor of Reims but known widely for his good works, sent her, shabbily dressed, to the house of friends who would shelter her. Young Mademoiselle Ponsardin married François Clicquot in 1799 in a wine cellar. All her life, she retained the same hairstyle –

The great Madame Clicquot, who was actually married in a cellar. (*Veuve Clicquot Ponsardin*)

corkscrew curls bunched over her ears. The Clicquots had one daughter but, in 1805, the young husband died. The widow decided to keep on running the business.

The tenacity of Madame Clicquot Ponsardin was matched by her remarkable ability to make associates of brilliantly astute businessmen. But she was at the centre – and in the cellar as well as driving over the vineyards. Her mind was ceaselessly active. The sediment in Champagne had, up to that time, been allowed to descend to the base of the bottle by the bottles being placed upside down in beds of sand. The young woman would go down into the cellars – lifts take visitors to those depths today – and, flicking her skirts away from the scurries of life that scampered from the light of her lamp, she walked and wondered and thought. And she evolved a series of holes, cut in the surface of her kitchen table, that could hold the bottles of wine and, gradually, tilt them so that the sediment might, gently, slide down to the base. With business preoccupations making demands on her, this 27-year-old woman, in spite of many setbacks, achieved the sort of success that, in today's parlance, makes her a star – in following her resolute motto 'One quality only – the finest!' (Summarised from *French Vintage*, Pamela Vandyke Price, 1986)

A CAPE LADY AND A WINE SNOB

Lady Anne Lindsay, a sensitive, creative person – she wrote the ballad 'Auld Robin Gray' – having had a disappointment in love, had resigned herself to not marrying until, when she was thirty-eight, she met and married Andrew Barnard, then only twenty-six. The marriage was idyllically successful. Barnard became Colonial Secretary in the Cape of Good Hope and Lady Anne went out to accompany him in 1797. Her notes and drawings enliven her letters but the charm of her personality emerges from all her writings, as when the ship in which the Barnards was travelling was threatened by a French vessel, Lady Anne prudently puts on two sets of underwear, and in the way she noted the 'salad garden' that the captain grew on board. When, at the Cape, the Barnards' cook was drunk at the first dinner they gave for the Governor, Lady Anne commented 'as I must often have laughed or cried, I thought it best to do the first.'

She was clear-sighted about how 'the Englishmen here turn up their noses at the Cape wines because they are Cape wines'. At one of her dinner parties she supposed the company to be drinking a little of the hock kept for 'Lord Macartney when he is ill', which she thought something special. (It had probably

189

benefitted from being cellared for some time.) She then comments that 'a certain lieutenant-colonel, who shall be nameless, on this filled his glass' and praised it. But when it was known that the wine was one of the local wines 'in a moment the colonel found fifty faults in it'.

Lady Anne went up Table Mountain twice – saying that, when her husband went with her on her second visit, she 'did the honours' for him. The Barnards spent two days and a night on the peak, seeing an eclipse of the sun.

Lady Anne's charm must have been obvious when she visited Constantia, because 'Mynheer Cloete', then in possession, didn't care for the British and was only rarely persuaded to let them buy any wine. But Lady Anne got to see the pressing 'where the whole of our party made wry faces at the idea of drinking wine that had been pressed from the grapes by three pairs of black feet; but the certainty that the fermentation would carry off any polluted particle settled that objection with me.' She noted how beautiful it was to see the 'three bronze figures' in the wine press.

SELECT BIBLIOGRAPHY

Place of publication London unless otherwise stated.

Adams, Leon. *The Wines of America*, Sidgwick and Jackson, 1984.

Ayto, John. *The Diner's Dictionary*, Oxford University Press, 1993.

Barty-King, Hugh. *A Tradition of English Wine*, Oxford University Press, Oxford, 1977.

Black, Maggie. *A Taste of History*, English Heritage, 1993.

Bradford, Sarah. *The Englishman's Wine: The Story of Port*, Macmillan, 1969.

Crawford, Anne. *History of the Vintners' Company*, Constable, 1977.

Edward, Gillian. *Hogmanay and Tiffany*, Geoffrey Bles, 1970.

Fielden, Christopher. 'Chaptal' in *Christie's Wine Companion*, 1989.

Gabler, James M. *Passions: The Wines and Travels of Thomas Jefferson*, Bacchus Press, Baltimore, 1995.

Hutchison, John N. *The Book of California Wine*, University of California Press and Sotheby's Publications, 1984.

Le Grand Livre des Confréries des Vins de France, Editions Dominique Halévy, Paris, 1971.

Mayson, Richard. *Portugal's Wine and Wine-makers*, Ebury, 1992.

Ordish, George. *The Great Wine Blight*, Dent, 1972.

Street, Julian. *Table Topics*, Cassell, 1959.

Vandyke Price, Pamela. *French Vintage*, Harrap, 1986.

Vandyke Price, Pamela, *Wine of the Graves*, Sotheby's, London, 1988.

INDEX

193

195